Anxious Souls Will Ask . . .

Anxious Souls Will Ask . . .

THE CHRIST-CENTERED SPIRITUALITY OF

Dietrich Bonhoeffer

John W. Matthews

William B. Eerdmans Publishing Company

Grand Rapids, Michigan / Cambridge, U.K.

© 2005 Wm. B. Eerdmans Publishing Co.
All rights reserved

Wm. B. Eerdmans Publishing Co.
255 Jefferson Ave. S.E., Grand Rapids, Michigan 49503 /
P.O. Box 163, Cambridge CB3 9PU U.K.

Printed in the United States of America

09 08 07 06 05   7 6 5 4 3 2

Library of Congress Cataloging-in-Publication Data

Matthews, John W., 1949-
Anxious souls will ask — the Christ-centered spirituality of Dietrich Bonhoeffer /
John W. Matthews.
p.   cm.
Includes bibliographical references.
ISBN 0-8028-2841-8 (pbk.: alk. paper)
1. Bonhoeffer, Dietrich, 1906-1945.   I. Title.

BX4827.B57M37   2005
230′.044′092 — dc22

2005041737

www.eerdmans.com

Contents

Contents

Foreword

Towards the end of the twentieth century, an impressive series of sculptures was added to the already magnificent treasury of sculptures adorning Westminster Abbey in London. This house of God records a long, multifaceted history through, among many other features, the stonework over the West Entrance to the Abbey. Men and women depicted in the new sculpture series are all twentieth-century persons, witnesses to God in life and work, and in sacrifice of even life itself. Their witness is to be remembered and commended in the labor of the sculptors who created figures of, among others, Oscar Romero, Martin Luther King, Jr., and Dietrich Bonhoeffer. Visitors learn from the guides at Westminster Abbey that everyone depicted there is considered a significant representative of the will of God for the whole of creation. Concerning Romero, King, and Bonhoeffer, one is left with the picture of three martyrs for truth, justice, and freedom. Not only are they worthy to be remembered as martyrs, it is good to allow oneself to be caught up by them into following Jesus Christ and embracing what Bonhoeffer called "costly grace."

Dietrich Bonhoeffer did not intend to become a martyr.

For him, seeking martyrdom was too much like trying to be a religious person, something he said we ought to give up trying to be. Read his letter of July 21, 1944, to Eberhard Bethge. There he refers to his earlier work *Discipleship*, written in 1937; the new critical edition in English was published under that title in 2001. In *Discipleship* he had developed reflections on what John Matthews calls "Christ-centered spirituality." The real issue for Bonhoeffer was that we so live with God and by God's grace that we will look for and follow after Jesus in our world, wherever that will take us, if necessary even unto our death. This is what Romero and King knew, the two men who stand at Bonhoeffer's right in the arch at Westminster Abbey and, like Bonhoeffer, who met violent death in their discipleship following Jesus.

The power of their martyrdom has touched John Matthews. As one commissioned and authorized by the church to make known the gospel of Jesus Christ, he is aware that his work requires much more than holding up "heroes of the faith" — what an odd way to portray faithful witnesses! Rather, people are to hear and be given what is promised to us and what it is we need for entering into the trust in God that will allow ourselves to be taken into discipleship. Such discipleship is that of the Christian witnesses to whom Westminster Abbey wants us to look. For the question is not: How do I become someone like King, Romero, or Bonhoeffer? Instead, we need to ask: How does their life, work, and witness help me in following Jesus in my here and now?

John Matthews calls attention to Bonhoeffer's remarkable collection of letters and papers from prison, so full of albeit fragmentary but very evocative ideas, in order to assist in the church's pastoral task today. This collection, called "Resistance and Surrender: Letters and Papers from Prison," has gone through a number of editions in German, each one expanding on the previous one and, since its first appearance in the early fifties of the last century, has been translated into numerous languages. The new, critical edition is soon to appear in English. Far more important and remarkable, however, is the impact that book has had. Here are some examples.

During the Seventh International Bonhoeffer Congress in Cape Town, January 1996, we learned while visiting the infamous Robben Island prison, where Nelson Mandela had been held for eighteen years, that Eberhard Bethge's biography of Dietrich Bonhoeffer had found its way — we were not told how — into that prison and that Mandela had more than likely read it. If that is true, what did he take from Bonhoeffer for his "long walk to freedom"? Why was the Dietrich Bonhoeffer Prize awarded in May 1999 to the Truth and Reconciliation Commission of South Africa, with Desmond Tutu himself coming to Berlin to accept the prize? Many of South Korea's Minjung theologians were arrested by the Korean CIA and imprisoned. Why did the Korean CIA prepare a "Bonhoeffer list" on which every arrested Minjung theologian's name was to be found? Why did thousands of Christians in that country, imprisoned by the Korean CIA during the bleak period of the military dictatorship, write the name of Dietrich Bonhoeffer in the confessions they were forced into composing? Why were these Christians so convinced that if martyrdom is the duty to resist and even to face death, it is the duty of the living and their responsibility to remember people like Bonhoeffer as they resist? What made Bonhoeffer and his book — it had been translated into Korean in 1965 — a dangerous memory of which to remember became a duty and responsibility? And what did the Minjung theologians and their students find in those letters that moved them to "liberate Jesus from the prison made by those who live for themselves only, the prison of the golden calf"? Such were the questions raised during a Bonhoeffer Lecture presented at Union Theological Seminary in New York on April 23, 1999. Finally, why did the leadership of the Protestant churches in the former German Democratic Republic turn to Dietrich Bonhoeffer in their search for ways of being the church there that refused restoration to pre-Nazi existence, that accepted and confessed the German churches' guilt of complicity in the horrors of the Third Reich? How did Bonhoeffer help them in their efforts to responsibly be a church neither against nor merely alongside, but within Socialism? What did they find that made them work on a political theology that resisted forgetting the past while also resisting the cheap grace of accommodation with the powers that be, however tempting that was? What did Christians of the GDR churches set out to build as a "church for others," as Gregory Baum puts it in his book with that title?

John Matthews knows this host of questions and many others like them and recognizes that all of them come from a context where Christians had turned to Bonhoeffer in their need to have what he calls "solid pillars" on which to rest. The realities of the world around them had pushed these Christians into a different, and to them hitherto unknown, territory where the familiar "pillars," or perhaps "flying buttresses," were found to be crumbling. But it is not answers to this host of questions that John Matthews is out to provide in this book. Instead, as a pastor, in our context here and now, he seeks to invite us to allow ourselves to be arrested by that figure over the entrance of Westminster Abbey and to be drawn into deep reflection on true discipleship for ourselves. I do not think it a coincidence that the planners of that series of sculptures placed Bonhoeffer and his fellow Christians *outside* the Abbey's walls. According to Bonhoeffer, to be the church, that is, to follow after Jesus Christ, is to follow him into the world rather than into the church. Such discipleship can no longer be held securely by many of the familiar, some say the "traditional" pillars of the Christian religion, as John Matthews sees it. He knows that for many a church member, returning to the "fleshpots of Egypt" — to use the image of Exodus 16:3 — is no option, and that moving into a promised but uncharted future can happen only if there is firm ground under our feet.

Bonhoeffer constructs no new pillars or buttresses; rather, in his reflections and the actions he undertook as one committed to Jesus Christ, he helps us in taking responsibility ourselves to stand on firm ground *and* move forward. This is the help John Matthews wants to offer in these pages: to engage Bonhoeffer and his prison correspondence and through engaging him, go with Bonhoeffer beyond Bonhoeffer into the freedom God gives us, the freedom that alone allows for our own genuine, that is, mature and responsible discipleship.

MARTIN RUMSCHEIDT

Acknowledgments

Any labor of significance involves a host of persons along the way who have contributed in one way or another to the shape and substance of a project. The following pages, being no exception, are the result of many experiences, significant reflection, and sustained discussion over many years with many persons. I want to take this opportunity to express my appreciation to some of these persons who have made a significant impact on my life and profoundly shaped the ministry I serve.

My wife, Patty, continues to be a source of strength and joy in all that I do. She has been an encouragement at every point, as well as a partner in dialogue on every issue and challenge I have faced. The life we share is a great source of inspiration from God that I will be thankful for all of my days.

My children, who number five, provide a constant source of wisdom and delight. From Sari, Maren, Bryan, Jodee, and Kayla I have received precious lessons for life.

In the summer of 1970, Dr. James Hofrenning at Concordia College encouraged my first serious study of the theology of Dietrich Bonhoeffer, and to him I will forever be grateful. Further study with Dr. James Burtness at Luther

Acknowledgments

Theological Seminary in 1971 cemented an interest and passion that, like my friendship with Jim, has only intensified over these thirty-four years. Involvement since 1975 in the International Bonhoeffer Society has resulted in numerous friendships of immense joy and deep commitment. These friends include Pat Kelley, Geff Kelly, Burton Nelson†, Martin Rumscheidt, Mark Randall, Guy Carter, Clifford Green, Mark Brocker, John Godsey, Wayne Floyd, Bill Peck, Charles Sensel, Gaylon Barker, Michael Lukens, Nancy Farrell, Lori Brandt-Hale, Jeff Pugh, Charles West, Martin Doblmeier, Robin Lovin, Larry Rasmussen, Mary Glazener, Clark Chapman, Eleanor Neel, Marlin and Sharon Johnson, Barry Harvey, Josiah U. Young III, Ruth Zerner, John de Gruchy, Vicki Barnett, Fritz de Lange, Andreas Pangritz, Ralf Wüstenberg, Gottfried Bretzger, Jane Pejsa, Keith Clements, Jean Bethke Elshtain, Alice Bond, Lee and Gary Blount, Lyn Holness, Dean Skelley, Peter Frick, Hans Pfeifer, Nancy Lukens, Lisa Dahill, Charles Marsh, and Renate Wind. Our mutual work to share the witness of Dietrich Bonhoeffer in a variety of ways, primarily academic, has been a rich life experience. Any list of thanks must include the friendship and support of Eberhard(†) and Renate Bethge, Bonhoeffer's friend/biographer and niece. Many of us in the Society have come to know the legacy of Bonhoeffer — almost firsthand — because of the generosity and labor of these two persons over the past five decades.

Books such as this one are often conceived, and just as often written, within a context that imprints itself on virtually every page. I am grateful to the members of Memorial Lutheran Church of Afton, Minnesota, for the opportunity of serving as their pastor from 1995 to 2003, and even more for the innumerable conversations that have strengthened my faith and deepened my reflection in the graciousness of God that we know in Jesus Christ. Since 2003 such conversation and reflection occurs primarily at Grace Lutheran Church of Apple Valley, Minnesota, the congregation I currently serve.

I close by quoting words of Dietrich Bonhoeffer that reflect my sentiments exactly regarding the work we do and the debt we owe to those who have gone before us:

> *Man überschätzt leicht das eigene Wirken und Tun in seiner Wichtigkeit gegenüber dem, was man nur durch andere Menschen geworden ist.*

> (We so easily overestimate our own work and action in its importance in comparison with what we have become only through others.)

Brief Chronology of Events

1906   Dietrich Bonhoeffer born in Breslau on February 4

1912   Karl Bonhoeffer (father) appointed as chair of the department of psychiatry and neurology at Kaiser Wilhelm University; family moves to Berlin

1923   Begins theological study at Tübingen

1924   Transfers to Kaiser Wilhelm University to continue study

1927   Receives Licentiate in Theology with the completion of *Sanctorum Communio*

1928   Spends one year as vicar for German parish in Barcelona, Spain

1930   Qualifies for teaching at Berlin University with *Act and Being* as his *Habilitationschrift*. In September leaves for one year of postgraduate study at Union Theological Seminary in New York City

1931   Returns to Berlin for teaching; appointed Youth Secretary of the World Alliance Conference at Cambridge; ordained November 15; teaches confirmation students at a church in Berlin-Wedding

1932   While teaching theology in Berlin, Bonhoeffer attends ecumenical meetings and prepares *Creation and Fall* for publication

1933   Adolf Hitler appointed Reich Chancellor on January 30; Nazi Boycott of Jewish businesses on April 1; Aryan Clause legislated; Bonhoeffer begins work with Martin Niemöller to form the Pastors' Emergency League; leaves in October for two-year parish ministry assignment in London

1934   Confessing Church established out of the Barmen Synod and Declaration; President Hindenburg dies in August and Hitler combines the two offices of Reich President and Reich Chancellor into one Reich Führer of the German people

1935   Bonhoeffer called back from London to direct one of five illegal (anti-Nazi) seminaries to train pastors of the Confessing Church, first located at Zingst, then at Finkenwalde

1936   Bonhoeffer forbidden to lecture at Kaiser Wilhelm University; visits Denmark and Sweden with students

1937   Martin Niemöller arrested July 1, which marks a low point in the morale of the Confessing Church; the seminary at Finkenwalde is closed by the Gestapo at the end of September

1938   Bonhoeffer begins conversation with those involved in the political resistance, learning the details of plans for conspiracy; *Life Together* written

1939   Conversations in March with Bishop George Bell, Reinhold Niebuhr, Gerhard Leibholz, and Visser 't Hooft in London; leaves Germany for New York City in June, but returns one month later, needing to live through this critical chapter of German history

1940   Recruited by his brother-in-law, Hans von Dohnanyi, to begin work as an agent of the German Military Intelligence and assigned to the Munich office of the Abwehr; he is forbidden to print or publish and is being watched by the Gestapo; while living in Munich, he often visits the Benedictine monastery at Ettal

1941   Participates in a rescue operation to assist Jews in leaving through Switzerland

1942   Makes "official" trips for the *Abwehr* to Switzerland, Norway, and Sweden

1943   Becomes engaged to Maria von Wedemeyer; arrested on April 5 and taken to Tegel prison in northwest Berlin

1944   Transferred to the Prinz Albrecht Strasse Gestapo Prison as a result of incriminating evidence found at Zossen regarding the unsuccessful plot on Hitler's life of July 20, 1944

1945   Transferred to Buchenwald KZ, then — via Regensburg and Schönberg — to Flossenbürg Concentration Camp and murdered there on April 9 with other key conspirators; also in April his brother Klaus and brothers-in-law Rüdiger Schleicher and Hans von Dohnanyi are murdered for conspiracy

April 30 Hitler commits suicide and on May 7 Germany surrenders

Preface

One of the primary purposes of religious belief is to provide a solid foundation and sturdy pillars for human beings as they seek to live their lives in this world meaningfully and securely. Individuals differ significantly as to how much meaning and security they need, as well as what kind of meaning and security they choose. Because religious belief serves this purpose of providing meaning and security, people can feel disoriented, respond defensively, and often their souls become anxious when the solid foundation or pillars of that belief are challenged or threatened. They feel insecure if crumbling pillars are pulled out from under them and others are not securely in place.

The German Lutheran pastor/theologian/martyr Dietrich Bonhoeffer is seen by many as sharing in the radical theological movement of the mid-twentieth century, whose purpose appeared to be pulling out familiar pillars of faith, challenging traditional notions of spirituality,[1] and even dismantling

---

1. The author is aware that Dietrich Bonhoeffer was cautious, if not critical, of using the word "spiritual" because of the inherent risk that it might be narrowly understood as merely the psychological feeling some

Christianity. In reality, the words and wisdom of Bonhoeffer, when more carefully understood rather than caricatured, point to very solid pillars of strength, clearly constructed on a solid foundation. However, because he does offer new insights regarding the content and meaning of Christian faith and spirituality, there will always be a risk of precipitating insecurity, meaning "anxious souls will ask . . ." (and worry) about the familiar pillars of faith and spirituality that appear to be challenged or threatened.

Unfortunately, the profound and provocative spiritual reflections found in the prison writings of Dietrich Bonhoeffer regarding the substance and shape of Christian faith and practice, as well as his observations about life in the modern world, have not yet become very well known, nor been generally affirmed throughout the church, since his untimely

---

persons claim to experience with God's presence (e.g., excitement, strength, certainty, power, purity). In the following pages "spiritual" and "spirituality" will be used to indicate the authentic (not contrived), deep (not superficial), total (not partial) experience of God's presence, always aware of Bonhoeffer's caution, yet employing a term that will no doubt continue to be used by Christian and non-Christian people for good and (unfortunately, at times) for bad. When the Lutheran Church in America, the American Lutheran Church, and the Association of Evangelical Lutheran Churches united in 1988, the intentional use of the word "evangelical" in their new name — Evangelical Lutheran Church in America — was an effort to reclaim and employ a significant biblical concept at the heart of the church's identity. Although the word "evangelical" had been primarily used by Christians of a more conservative orientation (from Schwärmer in Luther's time to charismatics in our time), those responsible for naming the ELCA affirmed in this decision the enduring value of an important mark of the church. Hence, to use the word "spiritual" or "spirituality" is to affirm the enduring value of these concepts in Christian vocabulary.

death in the spring of 1945. While Bonhoeffer's sacrificial life — like his academic tomes — have caught the attention of select audiences, his reflections regarding the substance of Christian faith and the shape of Christian spirituality that were crystallized during his imprisonment are considerably less known. In the following pages I intend to make these reflections more accessible and, I hope, more influential in the church today.

During the spring and summer months of Bonhoeffer's second year of Nazi imprisonment at the Tegel military prison in Berlin, his thoughts on the substance, shape, and meaning of Christianity intensified. In personal letters to his close friend and theological conversation partner, Eberhard Bethge, he offered reflections on and suggestions about authentic Christian discipleship. After the war, with the realization that Bonhoeffer's personal musings had profound implications for the future of the church and Christian spirituality, Bethge published those *Letters and Papers from Prison* in 1950,[2] little knowing that this private correspondence would, within a few decades, be recognized as a Christian classic.

Certainly, the publication of Anglican bishop John A. T. Robinson's *Honest to God* in 1963 (Philadelphia: Westminster Press) catapulted Bonhoeffer, along with Paul Tillich and Rudolf Bultmann, into the arena of popular religious discus-

---

2. Throughout the following pages, references will be made to Bonhoeffer's *Letters and Papers from Prison* by using dates only, so that locating a reference can be easily done, regardless of the particular edition used. The first Appendix includes selections from *Letters and Papers from Prison* (New York: Macmillan, 1972), for those wishing to make quick references to the correspondence from which the particular quotes are taken.

sion. Understandably, the criticism of traditional Christian theology and spirituality heard in these voices nourished the broader mood of discontent and turmoil then churning in America, culturally and religiously.

One context within which Bonhoeffer's prison writings were initially publicized and popularized was the radical theological movement of the 1960s, such as the short-lived "death of God" movement. The writings of Thomas J. J. Altizer, William Hamilton, and Paul M. van Buren (three well-known "death of God" theologians of that time) not only included quotations from Bonhoeffer's *Letters and Papers from Prison,* but explicitly acknowledged their indebtedness to, and inspiration from, the words and actions of Dietrich Bonhoeffer. As the "death of God" movement died, so did some of the initial interest in Bonhoeffer's theology, insofar as he was understood to be one of the sources for these radical views of Christianity.

At this same time, serious scholarly interest in the works of Bonhoeffer began in America with the publication of John Godsey's *The Theology of Dietrich Bonhoeffer* (London: SCM Press, 1960). It was then that more of Bonhoeffer's theological legacy became known (e.g., *The Communion of Saints, Act and Being, The Cost of Discipleship, Life Together, Ethics,* and his occasional sermons and lectures) and was found to have significant substance, deserving greater attention in the areas of Christology and ecclesiology. Also, a steady stream of doctoral dissertations, as well as books and journal articles, have continued to appear each year about the life and work of Dietrich Bonhoeffer. The understandable, yet unfortunate, reality is that most of the serious scholarship regarding

Bonhoeffer's legacy remains somewhat inaccessible to many persons because of its high level of theological-philosophical language and reflection. For that reason, much of the literary corpus of his legacy is neglected and, hence, lacks the visibility needed to inspire the church of our day.

I believe the greatest impact of Bonhoeffer's witness has come as a result of his martyrdom, his sacrificial offering of self for the cause of tyrannicide. Regardless of one's attitude toward Bonhoeffer's motives for becoming an accomplice with those conspiring to assassinate Hitler, his self-sacrifice is usually viewed with deep respect and stimulates inspiration. Many people moved by his example also seek out his writings, but often become frustrated with his difficult texts and challenged by his particularly ambiguous context. It is simply not easy for most people to digest much more than his *Life Together* or *Discipleship,* neither of which contains more than glimpses of the profound and provocative insights later developed in his prison writings. Hopefully, this book will serve the purpose of making the important theological texts of Dietrich Bonhoeffer, written from prison in the spring and summer of 1944, more accessible, and thus show clearly his Christ-centered spirituality.

Finally, let me add two observations about our context — in the first decade of the third millennium — that indicate why Bonhoeffer's reflections on Christian faith and spirituality are still relevant.

First, similar to the *world* that Dietrich Bonhoeffer inherited and interpreted, our world is also one in which there appears to be a high degree of secularity, with less interest for many people, not all, in the ways and wonders of God. Often,

Christian apologetics understands its role as criticizing the world's growing secularity in the hopes of reversing this tendency.

Dietrich Bonhoeffer sought to affirm both the ways and wonders of God and the secular maturation of the world, all with Jesus Christ at the center! We may do well to listen to his thoughts and entertain his suggestions.

Second, similar to the *church* that Dietrich Bonhoeffer inherited and interpreted, our church is also one that can often appear on the defensive. In the face of diminishing church membership and the (perceived) threat of religious pluralism, churches often resort to defensive tactics, attempting to show a world that feels little need for things religious of its real need for Jesus Christ. Much energy is spent in churches creating new and attractive programs in the hope of reducing their losses. It was in response to such a defensively postured church that Dietrich Bonhoeffer in 1944 reflected on authentic Christian discipleship. He did not propose to simply restore existing religious practices — which served to insulate people at the threatening edges of existence (death, shame and guilt, pain and loss) — but he rather suggested a faith-full "life for others," at the center of the God-given, present, secular life. Again, we may do well to listen and learn from his reflections.

As a Lutheran parish pastor, I have spent more than twenty-five years striving to integrate some of the profound and provocative insights of Dietrich Bonhoeffer with the experiences of the people I shepherd. While I have the theological tools necessary to whittle away at the legacy Bonhoeffer left, I am keenly aware that most of the people I serve do not and will not have such tools. I have personally remained involved in the academic realm of Bonhoeffer scholarship, while called to congregational ministry, in the hope of integrating theology and ministry, faith and life, the sacred with the secular.

It is my hope that in these pages we can reflect on the *world* we all experience, the *God* before whom we all finally must bow, and the *faith* required to positively affirm both *God* and the *world:* a faith and spirituality occasioned by, and known through, Jesus Christ. It is in this world, God, and faith that Dietrich Bonhoeffer lived and died.

God's People Embrace God's Future

In some respects the Christian church at the beginning of the third millennium CE resembles the faith community of Israel in 586 BCE (just prior to its exile), South Africa in 1988 CE (foreseeing its collapse as a country practicing apartheid), and the Eastern European Communist countries in 1989 (as the Iron Curtain was about to fall). Whenever collapse seems inevitable and demise likely, "anxious souls will ask . . ." about the shape that life among individuals and in community will take after the trauma, at times wondering whether there will even be a "life after." The despair and depression felt at such a time — personally and communally — result from anticipation that most of what has been known and cherished is threatened and will likely be taken away. The people of Israel in 586 BCE rightly perceived the Babylonian threat to mean the loss of their cherished temple, the center of their communal life. Attuned, and anxious, they naturally asked, "What will become of us?" As the pillars of the temple literally collapsed, there appeared to be for that ancient people no future, no hope, and for some, no God. Similarly, certain South Africans and Eastern Europeans experienced great anxiety as the foundations and pillars of their societies, even if repressive and hated by many, were crumbling.

The circumstances and details of loss and change vary with peoples and places, yet the dynamics of despair and depression remain remarkably consistent. Whether in ancient Israel or in modern Cape Town, whether Dresden in demise or Christendom in decline, "anxious souls will ask . . .," what is next to come?

While the Hebrew prophets claimed to speak from the divine perspective of an ultimate purpose for Israel's future (i.e., beyond the trauma and trials of exile), most folks despaired at the prospect of Babylonian captivity. As the Desmond Tutus claimed to speak from a divine perspective of equality and justice, and while Black and Afrikaner peoples in racially divided South Africa ultimately had much to gain from dismantling apartheid, those who in some way "benefited" from apartheid (the white minority) could not envision a more blessed future. At the beginning of the twenty-first century, with some shaking ecclesiastical foundations and crumbling theological pillars, Christendom is faced with the choice of embracing God's future with hope (a future that may well look quite different than the past) or attempting to restore the past, holding on tightly to what has been known and cherished. What has historically given strength to God's faithful people during times of trauma and transition has not so much been *what* they held on to from the past, but rather *who* they looked to for their present and future.

The biblical prophetic tradition existed to remind the people about God's earlier promises and acts of deliverance, to call them to trust God for a future beyond human imagination, and to make use of the present to examine themselves critically, moving into the future beyond the collapse. In sole dependence on the God of their covenant, the faithful were to endure and interpret the present, always in light of God's promise for a future. For sure, external forces of evil often contributed to the turbulent changes leading to collapse; yet the people of God were challenged to examine their own responsibility and lack of faithfulness for the destruction presently occurring.

The temptation of simply restoring things to a previous shape is usually safer and easier and therefore often preferred. "Conservative" is a word often used with restoration because both seek to preserve what was and ensure that it will continue to be. Simply restoring the past has a way of reducing anxiety about the future; whatever else one might say about the past, it is known, and such knowledge usually appears to promise greater security. "Anxious souls will ask . . ." about any future that begins to look somewhat different than the past.

The life and legacy of Dietrich Bonhoeffer offers a powerful, prophetic perspective for helping Christendom embrace God's future, without allowing anxiety to lure it toward simple, conservative restoration of the past. Born in the early part of the twentieth century, Bonhoeffer experienced the First World War as a child, seeing not only his country, but also Christendom, move from the center of European society to the edges. This decay caused him to examine and critique his society, always asking how God's promised future was to shape the present. Bonhoeffer's profound critique is overshadowed only by his powerful confidence in the grace of God for a church designed to serve God's future.

Dietrich Bonhoeffer —
Prophet of Truth and Transition

Born on February 4, 1906, in Breslau, Germany, to Karl and Paula Bonhoeffer, Dietrich Bonhoeffer was the sixth of eight children. Dr. Karl Bonhoeffer was, at the time of Dietrich's birth, a neurologist heading the psychiatric wing of the Charité Hospital in Breslau; Paula Bonhoeffer held the traditional domestic role of mother for the children, and with the help of governesses provided a secure and stimulating home environment. In 1912, the Bonhoeffer family moved to Berlin when Karl Bonhoeffer was appointed chair of the department of psychiatry and neurology at the Kaiser Wilhelm University. After living briefly near the Bellevue Station and then in the Grunewald district of Berlin where their neighbors included the Delbrucks, the von Harnacks, and the Plancks, they built a home in 1935 in Charlottenburg, which to this day stands and serves as a house of memorial and encounter.

Dietrich Bonhoeffer's parental home foundation offered an interesting "combination" of Christian piety and cautious agnosticism. From Dietrich's mother's family came a more traditional religious orientation; in addition to relatives who held responsible positions in church institutions (e.g., Karl

August von Hase, a court chaplain during Wilhelmian times), Paula was influenced by the Moravian Brethren governess working for them, Katie Horn. From Paula, the Bonhoeffer household received Christian piety through her prayers and religious observance, especially on holidays. From Karl Bonhoeffer's family came a more skeptical, scientific orientation; in spite of some relatives who were also involved in ecclesiastical circles, Karl Bonhoeffer, while being tolerant of those who did practice Christianity, was far more committed to a positivistic, pragmatic empiricism. Dietrich Bonhoeffer's decision to study theology, beginning at Tübingen in 1924, was affirmed by his mother and cautiously questioned by his father and older brothers. Told early on that a profession in the church would likely be uneventful and unimportant, Dietrich Bonhoeffer's life proved quite the opposite. He transferred after one year of study at Tübingen (1923-24) to the Kaiser Wilhelm University of Berlin, completing his doctorate in systematic theology in 1927. He was twenty-one years old. Clearly his innate abilities, as well as his family environment, help to explain the respect he would later receive.

A second significant "combination" relates to Bonhoeffer's educational foundation. Formally trained in twentieth-century liberal historical-critical disciplines, Bonhoeffer learned a scientific, empirical approach to theology, taught by persons whose names are now equated with liberal, modern, and scientific influence: Adolf von Harnack, Ernst Troeltsch, Hans Lietzmann, Reinhold Seeberg, Karl Holl, and Adolf Schlatter. Bonhoeffer was also captivated theologically by the neo-orthodox "crisis theology" of Reformed theologian Karl Barth. Although he never formally studied with

Barth, Bonhoeffer passionately absorbed the orientation of Barth's dialectical theological approach, while also laboring to affirm the contributions of his own liberal heritage. Bonhoeffer was keenly aware of each school's strengths and weaknesses. This "combination" of liberal and neo-orthodox training clearly shaped his theological orientation.

In 1934, when the anti-Nazi Pastors' Emergency League of two thousand clergy moved toward the Barmen Synod and the creation of an opposition Confessing Church, it was natural that Dietrich Bonhoeffer would be in the vanguard. With Karl Barth as the primary inspiration for, and author of, the famous Barmen Declaration, Bonhoeffer was close to the heart of Christian opposition to the growing malignancy of German Christianity as defined by the Nazis. The Confessing Church represented a significant opposing voice to the Nazi encroachment on the church's proclamation and practice until 1937, when its seminaries were officially closed and many of its leaders imprisoned. Martin Niemöller's arrest in July 1936 was a symbol of the National Socialists' resolve and capacity to silence the Protestant opposition within Hitler's Germany. It was at this low point that Bonhoeffer sought other channels for opposing the unchristian and inhumane reign of terror engulfing Europe.

Beginning in late 1937 and continuing into 1938, Dietrich Bonhoeffer became increasingly more knowledgeable of the resistance to Hitler developing within higher military echelons. Especially through his brothers-in law, Hans von Dohnanyi and Rüdiger Schleicher, and his brother, Klaus, he came to see the necessity of, and the mechanism for, tyrannicide to end Germany's aggressive war against nations, the

Jews, and other "undesirables." He was formally commissioned in 1939 by German military intelligence — the *Abwehr* — as an agent who would "officially" travel to other countries promoting Germany's "honor and good intentions" while simultaneously (and clandestinely) sharing information with the Allies about the attempted coup in process among the military generals. The focus of Bonhoeffer's travel was to engender respect and gain support for a new German leadership, already chosen and thoroughly trustworthy, to be put in place immediately following a successful plot to assassinate Hitler. As we know, the Allies did receive the information and plans for the conspiracy — sent through Bonhoeffer and others — but summarily refused to act sympathetically, reaffirming that nothing short of total surrender by the Axis powers would be acceptable.

Bonhoeffer was imprisoned in April 1943 on suspicion of helping save some Jews by using *Abwehr* connections to open their way for escape to Switzerland. For eighteen months he was confined in Berlin's Tegel military prison, receiving some family visits and letters. After the unsuccessful attempt to assassinate Hitler on July 20, 1944, and the subsequent discovery of incriminating evidence in the *Abwehr* files at Zossen, Bonhoeffer was moved to a higher-security prison at the Prinz Albrecht Strasse Gestapo Headquarters. Virtually all communication with the outside world was then cut off, as Nazi paranoia and the Allied pressure continued to increase. In the final days of the war, Bonhoeffer was taken to the Buchenwald KZ, then Regensburg, Schönberg, and finally the Flossenbürg KZ, the place of his death. On April 9, 1945, he and several other key persons involved in the conspiracy were put to death by hanging, only two weeks before the Allied forces arrived to liberate that concentration camp.

Bonhoeffer's life and witness have been challenges for many attempting to understand how such a committed Christian — even a pacifist in his earlier days — could become an accomplice with conspirators, and finally appearing to suffer a humiliating traitor's death. His radical reflections from Tegel prison about a "world-come-of-age" and his "non-religious interpretation of Biblical concepts" have tended to amplify this challenge. For sure, Bonhoeffer's heroic sacrifice elicits respect and inspiration. Unfortunately, these rather obvious public glimpses of his character leave untouched the most profound, and potentially helpful, parts of his legacy: his embracing of God's presence and future without allowing anxiety from a crumbling world and church to lure him and his vision for Christendom towards a simple, conservative restoration of the past. It is in his prison letters to Eberhard Bethge during the spring and summer of 1944 that Bonhoeffer critiqued his inherited Christian tradition and offered profound and prophetic observations about the world and suggestions for the church. With this brief sketch of his life and witness, we now proceed to examine more closely the reflections of a man whose love for God and embrace of the world coalesced in an authentic Christian faith that can serve as a model in the present and into the future. It will be made clear, I hope, just how Christ-centered the spirituality of this modern man really was.

CHAPTER I

The Solid Foundation

The life and legacy of Dietrich Bonhoeffer witness profoundly to a Christ-centered vision of the reality of God
in the church and in the world. A very solid christological-
theological foundation is clearly evident in all that he said
and wrote. Yet, in a letter dated July 16, 1944, Dietrich
Bonhoeffer wrote from prison to his good friend and theological conversation partner, Eberhard Bethge, of his awareness that in speaking of some new ways about Christian
faith, "Anxious souls will ask what room there is now left for
God. . . ."

It is very important to remember that Bonhoeffer's theological reflections during the time of his imprisonment by
the Nazis (1943-1945) were essentially fragmentary and not
organized as topics for lectures or written as paragraphs for
inspirational literature. When Eberhard Bethge, in 1950, de-
cided to publish Bonhoeffer's *Letters and Papers from Prison*
(Widerstand und Ergebung), they were assembled, as nearly as
possible, in chronological order, without a particular ar-
rangement of topics or themes. For this reason, the letters
written during the spring and summer of 1944 include a dynamic mixture of reflections by Bonhoeffer that are, in part,

positive and constructive and, in part, negative and critical. Often spoken in an academic tone, these profound insights and practical suggestions, which could be so important for our church today in its striving for authentic spirituality and witness, are often overlooked. The quote above, which includes within it the title of this book, reveals that Bonhoeffer was keenly aware that some of his reflections about God, the world, the church, and Christian faith might possibly upset people, causing them to wonder whether everything familiar and secure was up for grabs. My sense is that many people who begin to read these profound — yet challenging — reflections of Bonhoeffer become anxious, concluding prematurely that he had abandoned his Christian faith. My hope is that by organizing the prison reflections, beginning with the solid foundation, we will not only more fully appreciate his positive contribution, but subsequently come to understand the meaning of, and reason for, his critical comments. Now some sixty years after his martyrdom, with most of the personal, historical, and theological legacy of Dietrich Bonhoeffer well documented, we are at a place to assemble and organize that which he did not have the luxury or longevity to do. We will ultimately respect his life and honor his death most by weaving the diverse threads of his witness into one beautiful tapestry, always knowing that some strands read in isolation may mean that "Anxious souls will ask. . . ." As experienced weavers we must patiently wait until the entire work is woven (that is, understood). Let us look then to Bonhoeffer's theological reflections . . . beginning with his solid foundation!

Who Is Jesus Christ for Us Today?

Although bits and pieces of serious theological reflection can be read in the correspondence of Dietrich Bonhoeffer during his first year of confinement at Tegel prison, it is in his letter of April 30, 1944, to Eberhard Bethge that he began a more sustained and focused conversation. Two questions that he asked in that letter bring into sharp relief the constructive and critical musings he entertained: "What Christianity really is, or indeed who Christ really is, for us today." Bonhoeffer had a passionate interest in experiencing God's presence in his (Bonhoeffer's) particular time and place. This passion was fundamental to all that he thought and wrote. In the same letter of April 30 he asked related questions:

> What do a church, a community, a sermon, a liturgy, a Christian life mean . . . ? How do we speak of "God"? . . . What is the meaning of worship and prayer . . . ?

It will be important for us, as we inquire about Dietrich Bonhoeffer's theology and spirituality, to understand that these questions are not casual, flippant, or cynical, based on some desire to discount, discredit, or diminish the ways God and Christ and faith had been experienced. Rather, he was taking God's incarnate presence in Jesus Christ so seriously that he sought ever new and dynamic ways of knowing, believing, and following Christ in the present.

> I should like to speak of God not on the boundaries but at the centre, not in weakness but in strength; and

therefore not in death and guilt but in one's life and goodness. . . . God is beyond in the midst of our life. The church stands, not at the boundaries where human powers give out, but in the middle of the village. . . . How this . . . looks, what form it takes, is something that I'm thinking about a great deal.

For sure, the omnipresent, omnipotent, omniscient God of Christian tradition was known and presupposed by Bonhoeffer when he here inquired about ever deeper experiences of faith. However, insofar as Christian tradition over time had come to focus more on God's omnipresence experienced primarily at life's boundaries, and God's omnipotence experienced mostly in life's moments of weakness, and God's omniscience usually experienced when dealing with issues of death and guilt, Bonhoeffer here wanted "to speak of God . . . [also] at the centre, . . . in strength . . . in one's life and goodness." In fact, Bonhoeffer, who was (unfortunately) later to be accused of preaching the "death of God," was here claiming even *more* reality for God. In addition to the more traditional places and spaces reserved for God (i.e., life's boundaries, human weakness, and the guilt often felt by people), he wished to emphasize God's presence at the center, in strength, near the goodness of human existence. Bonhoeffer is suggesting an even more expansive view of the Lordship of Jesus Christ. Again, he is not a cynic out to destroy, but a critic out to deepen! These radical questions are intended to inspire, not to incite.

The solid foundation on which Bonhoeffer wished to stand was first and finally the God of Abraham and Sarah and the father of Jesus Christ, as attested in Holy Scripture and experienced in the church.

Moving forward chronologically from this first "theological" letter, we are soon enjoying the beautiful "Thoughts on the Day of the Baptism of Dietrich Wilhelm Rüdiger Bethge," a sermon prepared — and then sent from his prison cell at Tegel — for the May 21, 1944, baptism of his godson. In earlier letters to Eberhard Bethge, Bonhoeffer mentioned his excitement over Bethge's child being his (Dietrich's) namesake, as well as his sadness that he would not be able to be present for the blessed event because of his imprisonment. In the baptismal sermon Bonhoeffer wrote:

> Today you (Dietrich Bethge) will be baptized a Christian. All those great ancient words of the Christian proclamation will be spoken over you, and the command of Jesus Christ to baptize will be carried out on you, without your knowing anything about it. But we are once again being driven back to the beginnings of our understanding. Reconciliation and redemption, regeneration and the Holy Spirit, love of our enemies, cross and resurrection, life in Christ and Christian discipleship — all these things are so difficult and so remote that we hardly venture any more to speak of them. . . . Our church, which has been fighting in these years only for its self-preservation, as though that were an end in itself, is incapable of taking the word of reconciliation and redemption to mankind and the world. Our earlier words are therefore bound to lose their force and cease, and our being Christians today will be

limited to two things: prayer and righteous action among people.

Bonhoeffer was keenly aware that on the solid foundation of the "great ancient words of the Christian proclamation" stood the particular form (the pillars) that Jesus Christ must assume for God's redeeming presence to be known. Here, in a sermon designed to bless the faithful who were to gather for a baptism, Dietrich Bonhoeffer shared critical words of prophetic impulse, words against Christ's church because — in his opinion — reconciliation and redemption in the world were being hindered by a church "fighting in these years only for its self-preservation." And from here he proposed a posture and a plan for "being Christians . . . there will be those who pray and do right and wait for God's own time."

Already in this sermon of May 1944, one can discern his criticism of traditional words that had lost their power (e.g., reconciliation, redemption, regeneration, cross, resurrection, discipleship), criticism offered in an effort to prepare the way for a more authentic speaking/acting-out of God's presence. Slightly more than a week after the baptism of Dietrich Bethge, Bonhoeffer's reflections on "Who Christ really is for us today" began to include more and more talk of God's presence in Christ in the world. On May 29, 1944, after a brief excursus on the multidimensional aspects of Christian life, he wrote:

We are to find God in what we know, not in what we don't know; God wants us to realize his presence, not in unsolved problems but in those that are solved. . . . God is no stop-gap; he must be recognized at the centre of life . . . not only when death comes; in health and vigor, and not only in suffering; in our activities, and not only in sin. The ground for this lies in the revelation of God in Jesus Christ. He is the centre of life.

And later, on June 27, Bonhoeffer wrote: "Christ takes hold of a person at the centre of his life." The thoughts and concerns stated earlier in the April 30th letter continued and were expanded so that persons experience God "in what we know," in problems "that are solved . . . in health and vigor . . . in our activities." Again, Bonhoeffer is suggesting a more expansive (not less expansive) view of the Lordship of Jesus Christ.

In early July 1944, Bonhoeffer wrote a poem, "Christians and Pagans," drawing together in three verses not only his understanding of how Christian discipleship differed from generic religious practice, but also what constituted the very core of Christian identity and vocation. I include the German original of this poem, so that those desiring to compare it to any English translation will have it close at hand:

Christen und Heiden

Menschen gehen zu Gott in ihrer Not,
flehen um Hilfe, bitten um Glück und Brot,
um Errettung aus Krankheit, Schuld und Tod.
So tun sie alle, alle, Christen und Heiden.

Menschen gehen zu Gott in Seiner Not,
Finden ihn arm, geschmäht, ohne Obdach und Brot,

sehn ihn verschlungen von Sünde, Schwachheit und Tod.
Christen stehen bei Gott in Seinen Leiden.

Gott geht zu allen Menschen in ihrer Not,
sättigt den Leib und die Seele mit Seinem Brot,
stirbt für Christen und Heiden den Kreuzestod,
und vergibt ihnen beiden.

I have personally translated Bonhoeffer's poem, reordering
the second and third verses and adding a final verse, as well as
composing music for the words, so this profound piece of
Christian literature can be used for worship. In my estima-
tion, no clearer words were ever written by Dietrich Bonhoeffer to express his conviction about the substance and
shape, the content and meaning of Christian spirituality and
discipleship.

It was during the month of July 1944 that Bonhoeffer's
reflections turned ever more specifically toward the unique-
ness of Christian discipleship, compared to most other
forms of religiosity. In his mind, as the words of his poem
"Christen und Heiden" reveal, most human beings look to
God as a source of strength in their weakness and for help
in time of trouble; one need not be Christian to believe in
God and look to the Almighty for aid in times of great need.
Bonhoeffer observed that for many Christian people — no
different than pagans — religious belief amounted to little
more than tipping one's hat to a divine power, and then,
mostly out of fear, offering obeisance and token gestures of
respect, all in hope of relying on God's help when needed.
His evolving understanding of Christian discipleship came

Christians Stand by God

Text: Dietrich Bonhoeffer, 1906-1945

Tune & text adaptation: John W. Matthews

Peo - ple go to God when they are sore____ be - stead,
God goes out to ev' - ry one when sore____ be - stead,
We are called to find the pla - ces God is sore be - stead,
Lord, help us to look for you in those who are be - stead,

Beg - ging God for suc - cor, want - ing peace and dai - ly bread.
Feed - ing bod - ies, spir - its of - fer - ing the liv - ing bread.
In our poor, neg - lec - ted neigh - bors with - out home or bread.
In the lives of bro - ken peo - ple, seek - ing peace and bread.

That they might be saved from sick - ness, freed from sin and death,
Chris - tians, like all oth - ers, loved by God who hangs there dead,
Ov - er - come by grief God bears all sin, and pain, and death.
Where you are we wish to meet you, streng - then us, O Lord,

Chris -tians, like all oth - ers ask that God would be their stead.____
Of - fer - ing, for - giv - ing, sac - ri - fi - cing in their stead.____
Chris - tians are to stand by God and suf - fer in God's stead.____
To be Christ for oth - ers, bring - ing wa - ter and the Word.____

to mean not primarily what a divine power could be called upon to do for humans, but what humans are called upon to do for God! In this context, he wrote to Bethge on July 16th:

> Religiosity makes one look in distress to the power of God in the world. . . . The Bible directs one to God's powerlessness and suffering.

Two days later he wrote:

> The poem about Christians and pagans contains an idea that you will recognize: "Christians stand by God in his hour of grieving"; that is what distinguishes Christians from pagans. . . . One is summoned to share in God's sufferings at the hands of a godless world. . . . It is not the religious act that makes the Christian, but participation in the sufferings of God . . . not in the first place thinking about one's own needs, problems, sins, and fears, but allowing oneself to be caught up into the way of Jesus Christ.

Ironically, for many Christians, the call to discipleship (humans sharing in God's suffering as Jesus did) has been misconstrued to mean a road taken with God to avoid suffering. While a desire for guardianship by (some) god for protection from the brokenness and bestiality of the world is understandable, it does not, for Bonhoeffer, constitute Christian discipleship. This kind of desperate clinging to God is characterized in (his criticism of) the notion of a *deus ex machina*, a "god of the machine," such as was used in ancient Greek drama to rescue persons from impossible life situations. So, quite contrary to leaning on a god who simply guards one from pain and suffering, the disciple of Jesus walks with a God who experiences pain and suffering and then engages it. We sense that, in contrast to the usual religious question about the "usefulness of God" for people, Bonhoeffer preferred to speak of Christian spirituality and discipleship as the "usefulness of humans" for God!

In this profound poem, "Christians and Pagans," like the reflections of July 16 and 18, Bonhoeffer lifted up the solid foundation of Christian faith and life: Jesus Christ himself. However, Bonhoeffer labored hard to ensure that the Lord whom Christians follow is the Crucified One (Jesus Christ), who invites persons to participate with God *in* the world, not a lord of human invention sought to extricate one *from* the world.

As the solid foundation on which Bonhoeffer stands is first, and finally, the God known in Jesus Christ, as attested in the Scriptures and experienced in the church, so now we see this foundation is established in a broken world in which God suffers and in which the disciples of Jesus Christ are called to fully participate.

On the day following the unsuccessful attempt to assassinate Adolf Hitler (July 20, 1944), Dietrich Bonhoeffer wrote words that reveal his deep passion for experiencing and understanding the reality of God, even through times when the "powerful" hands of God seemed to be tied. Aware on July 21, 1944, of the failure of the conspirators to end the totalitarian reign of terror by ending the life of the evil tyrant in charge,

Bonhoeffer searched deeper than ever for signs of God's presence. He wrote:

> I mean living unreservedly in life's duties, problems, successes and failures, experiences and perplexities. In so doing we throw ourselves completely into the arms of God, taking seriously, not our own sufferings, but those of God in the world — watching with Christ in Gethsemane.

In faithful trust he concluded his letter with these words: "May God in his mercy lead us through these times; but above all, may he lead us to himself."

One could easily understand, given the circumstances of life in Tegel prison and news of the failure of the July 20th plot on Hitler's life, if Dietrich Bonhoeffer had been able to dwell only on people's misery and the hopelessness of his situation. Given the uncertainty of each day, the abuse and torture of human beings, and the apparent victory of evil in so many ways, how could one expect any sincere optimism or balance in perspective? Yet, he wrote that "one learns to have faith . . . by living unreservedly in life's duties, problems, successes and failures, experiences and perplexities."

The solid foundation — God in Jesus Christ — is established in a troubled world in which God suffers! Christian discipleship then is to "throw ourselves completely into the arms of God" and living "unreservedly in life." The solid foundation, Jesus Christ, is God incarnationally present in every nook and cranny of existence, within which his disciples are called to participate.

One additional entry in Bonhoeffer's *Letters and Papers from Prison* is worth noting regarding his vision for responsible Christian spirituality and discipleship. In a proposed "Outline for a Book" (summer 1944), many of his ideas sketched out earlier and sporadically in letters to Bethge were assembled and ordered. In that outline, while never completed, we see Bonhoeffer's (sociological) observations about the church and the world, his (theological) convictions about Christian faith in the days to follow, and his (ethical) prescriptions for responsible Christian discipleship in the world. He wrote:

> Faith is participation in this being of Jesus (incarnation, cross, and resurrection). Our relation to God is not a "religious" relationship to the highest, most powerful, and best Being imaginable — that is not authentic transcendence — but our relation to God is a new life in "existence for others," through participation in the being of Jesus. The transcendental is not infinite and unattainable tasks, but the neighbor who is within reach in any given situation. . . . The church is the church only when it exists for others. . . . The church must share in the secular problems of ordinary human life, not dominating, but helping and serving.

In these beautiful words, wise and passionate, Bonhoeffer gave us an image — an answer — for his life question, "Who is Christ really for us today?" Completing a trajectory of some seventeen years, his words from *Sanctorum Communio* are repeated, yet amplified, and so much fuller because of his life experience. He wrote in 1927, "This being-with-each-other of the church community and its members through Christ already entails their being-for-each-other."[1] In 1944 he wrote, "Jesus is there only for others . . . the church is the church only when it exists for others."

"Who is Jesus Christ for us today?" Eberhard Bethge later wrote about this:

> And thus Bonhoeffer, as we have already said, added a new title to the old ones of Jesus, one that is both intelligible and at the same time profound: "The man for others." . . . This Christological title of honor, "the man for others," is confession, hymn, prayer and interpretation.[2]

And, hence, for those who "participate in the being of Jesus" and "share in the sufferings of God in the world," they will "exist for others" ("Outline for a Book").

Near the end of 1944, and in one of the last pieces of correspondence Bonhoeffer sent from Tegel prison, he wrote beautiful verses about trusting God as well as accepting consequences of faithful obedience. In "Powers of Good" we find phrases such as "thankfully receiving all that is given by thy loving hand"; "should it be thy will"; "boldly we'll face the future, come what may"; and "God will befriend us." The words below were written after twenty months of prison confinement and deep reflection, revealing that he not only

1. Dietrich Bonhoeffer, *Sanctorum Communio*, vol. 1 (Minneapolis: Fortress Press, 1998), p. 182.
2. Eberhard Bethge, *Dietrich Bonhoeffer — Man of Vision, Man of Courage* (New York: Harper and Row, 1970), p. 790.

sought the presence of God in vitality and action, but also desired to understand the presence of God in solitude and resignation.

Powers of Good

With every power for good to stay and guide me,
comforted and inspired beyond all fear,
I'll live these days with you in thought beside me,
and pass, with you, into the coming year.

The old year still torments our hearts, unhastening;
the long days of our sorrow still endure;
Father, grant to the souls thou hast been chastening
that thou hast promised, the healing and the cure.

Should it be ours to drain the cup of grieving
even to the dregs of pain, at thy command,
we will not falter, thankfully receiving
all that is given by thy loving hand.

But should it be thy will once more to release us
to life's enjoyment and its good sunshine,
that which we've learned from sorrow shall increase us,
and all our life be dedicate as thine.

Today, let candles shed their radiant greeting;
lo, on our darkness are they not thy light
leading us, haply, to our longed-for meeting? —
Thou canst illumine even our darkest night.

When now the silence deepens for our hearkening,
grant we may hear thy children's voices raise
from all the unseen world around us darkening
their universal paean, in thy praise.

While all the powers of good aid and attend us,
boldly we'll face the future, come what may.
At even and at morn God will befriend us,
and oh, most surely on each newborn day!

— December 1944 —

CHAPTER II

The Crumbling Pillars

I t was while Dietrich Bonhoeffer stood firmly upon the solid foundation of God, known and experienced through the incarnate, crucified, and present Jesus Christ, that he thought about the world in which he lived and the church he served. In several ways similar to our experience entering the twenty-first century, Bonhoeffer understood that the modern world of science and technology was experiencing greater and greater self-confidence, a kind of "defection from God." The practice of religion was clearly on the decline, and the church — as an institution — was becoming less and less influential. As the Western world's self-understanding changed, the church's traditional concepts and confessions had become less and less meaningful, or at least anachronistic. As traditional Christian faith came into conflict with modern science and technology, the former was often found wanting and then unconsciously — if not consciously — retired. Bonhoeffer, among others, saw that more and more of the world was being investigated, questioned, quantified, classified, and managed without recourse to God and traditional religious concepts. Unlike many of his contemporaries, he chose to accept the challenge of addressing the world's question to the church of the twentieth century: "What room is there left for God now?" (July 16, 1944). Bonhoeffer was certainly aware that one way of meeting the challenge would have been to retreat defensively behind the religious answers, traditional concepts, and faith pillars of earlier days; he chose not to do this. And so, in the same letter quoted earlier (April 30, 1944) he asked, "How can Christ become the Lord of the religionless?" Rather than fault the world for asking questions, derived from ever-increasing knowledge, he chose to critique the church for dispensing outdated answers that seemed less than honest and not very helpful. While many factors contributed to Bonhoeffer's willingness to accept this challenge of secular society, certainly his agnostic father, brothers, and brothers-in-law played a significant role in prompting him to "give reason for the faith that lies within." Years earlier, when accused of committing his life and labors to an institution that was "antiquated and useless," he responded that if the church was feeble, "I shall reform it!"[1] Dietrich Bonhoeffer agreed with those who thought that some traditional "religious" pillars of Christian faith (i.e., privilege, a pre-modern scientific outlook, individualistic spirituality, pre-critical biblical hermeneutics) were crumbling in the face of modernity; he also knew that the solid Christian foundation (God, Christ, church, salvation, resurrection, et al.) had not essentially shifted.

Having defined the solid Christian foundation upon which the church stands, Bonhoeffer turned to the crum-

---

1. Eberhard Bethge, *Dietrich Bonhoeffer — Man of Vision, Man of Courage* (New York: Harper and Row, 1970), p. 22.

bling pillars he thought needed replacement. Again, we begin with that first "theological" letter from prison of April 30, 1944.

> You would be surprised, and perhaps even worried, by my theological thoughts and the conclusions they lead to. . . . We are moving towards a completely religionless time; . . . what does that mean for "Christianity"? It means that the foundation is taken away from the whole of what has been up to now our "Christianity."

Bonhoeffer's critique of religion (better, the "religious *a priori* of mankind") began here to unfold as he reflected on the apparent condition of church and world: "People as they are now simply cannot be religious anymore." As we begin to examine the crumbling pillars, it is imperative we understand what Bonhoeffer meant by the term "religion," for the pillars needing replacement all somehow fall under what he called "religion."

For most people, "religion" is a belief system with positive moral principles that creates a genuine reverence for life and a healthy force for social cohesion. If, and when, more fanatical belief systems encourage values other than these, people tend to use a word such as "cult" to distinguish them from authentic religion. It should be noted that Bonhoeffer does not equate Christian faith with what he calls "religion." Karl Barth, one of Dietrich Bonhoeffer's theological mentors, also differentiated Christian faith from generic religion. For Barth, the Christian proclamation is that God — in Christ — has reached "down" to rescue humanity, a gracious and divine act independent of any human effort. In contrast, religion, according to Barth and then Bonhoeffer, was understood to be any human activity, however sincere, that reaches "up" or strives to reach or control God. Bonhoeffer's negative comments about religion are not a rejection of God, Christ, church, salvation, resurrection, etc. When he refers to "religion" as a passing thing that many people can no longer endorse, he means something very particular. Eberhard Bethge, in his splendid biography *Dietrich Bonhoeffer — Man of Vision, Man of Courage,* summarized what "religion" meant for Bonhoeffer: individualism, metaphysics, partiality, privilege, and dependence. In short, Bonhoeffer came to understand these elements, commonly understood as "religious," as unhelpful pillars that were crumbling and not essential to Christian discipleship and spirituality.

First, while Christian faith is most certainly personal, involving a relationship between God and particular human beings, Bonhoeffer believed as early as his doctoral dissertation, *The Communion of Saints* (1927), that the church is "Christ existing as community." Therefore, individual, private, inward acts and gestures may be termed "religious" but hardly comprise the full spectrum of Christian spirituality, which is also profoundly communal. Bonhoeffer, while resonating with some of Rudolf Bultmann's exegetical insights, did not affirm the individualism often equated with existential philosophy and faith. Likewise, he was critical of Methodism's traditional appeal to individual inward experience as the essence of Christian faith. Bonhoeffer understood that Christ's present form was essentially communal and that one who lived "in Christ" necessarily lived in community. This understanding of the corporate dimension of Christian life only intensified as Bonhoeffer's life developed. Therefore, his critique of this aspect of religion — individualism — is not a criticism of the personal but of the private emphasis of some spirituality.

Second, as early as *The Communion of Saints,* Bonhoeffer labored to demonstrate that the metaphysical quality of divine "otherness," which seems to be such an important characteristic of God for "religion," is overshadowed within Christian theology and spirituality by God's nearness in the incarnation, Jesus Christ. His critique of traditional Christian metaphysics was because God then was portrayed as being "painfully distant." That God became man, through the incarnation of Jesus Christ, reveals God's desire to draw close to humanity, something that gods are not usually known to do. Bonhoeffer's embracing of a *theologia crucis* (theology of the cross) is related to his criticism of religion's metaphysical God of "otherness." While acknowledging that God is beyond and distant, Bonhoeffer also contended that God in Christ has also drawn near. Any spirituality that keeps God only remote may be "religious" but not, according to Bonhoeffer, Christian.

Third, one discovers that Bonhoeffer's understanding of "religion" included the notion that God was known and experienced only in certain parts of life, in partiality. In a manner reminiscent of Persian dualism, the divine presence was mostly something experienced in prayer, worship, meditation, etc. Religious practice tended to foster distance from the world and such "dark places" as politics, labor, commerce, and the arts. Against this "religious" separation, or partition, of reality into good and bad, light and dark, spiritual and worldly, Bonhoeffer affirmed the incarnate God — in Christ — present in all of reality. For him, there were not multiple spheres of life, some divine and others not; rather, in Christ, all of life was claimed and occupied by God! Therefore, his critique of this aspect of religion — partiality — opens the way for God's redeeming presence in all of life, not simply in those places and spaces humans call good that deserve divine endorsement.

Fourth, we discover that the "theology of the cross" (central to Martin Luther's theological orientation) was also at the heart of Bonhoeffer's critique of the privileged quality of "religion." His judgment was that Christian people move away from Christ, in some sense, when they hide behind or seek protection in society's privilege. Early examples of this were Constantine's and Theodosius' edicts in 313 CE and 380 CE, offering the persecuted followers of Jesus official, protected status within the empire. Bonhoeffer saw the German (state) church in all its glory as an establishment of privilege; "religion" was being practiced, but following the Crucified One was missing! His book, *The Cost of Discipleship (Nachfolge)*, most clearly addressed this particular critique of "religion." Similar to Abraham and Sarah's blessing from Yahweh to be blessings for others, the followers of Jesus were called to service, not to privilege.

Finally, and perhaps most difficult to grasp initially, is that characteristic of "religion" Bonhoeffer referred to as dependence. He is not here criticizing a legitimate recognition and gratitude by humans that all one has comes from the hand of God. Of course, it does! The dependence of which he speaks is an immature overdependency, leaning on God for things human beings are very capable of and should be doing for themselves and others. As people physically and emotionally grow from infancy to adolescence to adulthood, so ought they grow and mature spiritually, in faith. While tutelage is an understood thing for those who are young, immature, and growing, the goal for those who are mature should be responsible interdependence. That Christian people could and should be mature was not to suggest, for Bonhoeffer, that a state of moral or spiritual perfection was then achieved. Rather, maturity would mean thinking, deciding, and acting responsibly, having grown beyond adolescent dependency on one's parent or tutor or God(!) for answers, permission, or detailed direction. Today, we might say that God is not interested in micromanaging the things that humans can and should be doing for themselves. People have always been called to be responsible stewards of God's creation. While human overdependence on God may seem "religiously" admirable, it was, for Bonhoeffer, a false understanding of mature spirituality and Christian discipleship.

Bonhoeffer's conviction was that these "religious" elements, often equated with Christian faith, were outdated, crumbling pillars of a bygone time, mentality, and orientation. In place of individualistic, metaphysical, partial, privileged, and dependent (i.e., "religious") ways of experiencing God's presence, he wished to emphasize these theological/faith pillars: "Christ existing as community"; "God as the beyond in our midst"; "God claiming the whole world"; "Christian faith as life lived for others"; and a "world come of age." Whereas "religious" pillars certainly characterized and supported people's faith in days past, he thought the time had arrived for interpreting Christ's presence "non-religiously." Bonhoeffer's demolishing of outdated pillars of "religion" was ultimately for the purpose of erecting new and relevant pillars for Christian faith in the future . . . all built to lift up, support, and witness to the eternal, biblical God, incarnate in Jesus Christ!

CHAPTER III

The New Pillars Needed

To replace the crumbling pillars of the Christian tradition that he saw collapsing, Bonhoeffer suggested new pillars for the church of the future. Far from obscuring or distorting the solid foundation upon which the church is grounded, Bonhoeffer's "creative fidelity" (the words of Charles Curran) offers both continuity with the past and challenge for the future. Woven within the letters to Eberhard Bethge in the spring and summer of 1944 from Tegel prison are profoundly new concepts that can assist the church, as well as the secular world, in experiencing the eternal, authentic, ever-contemporary presence of God.

Pillar #1

On May 5, 1944, Dietrich Bonhoeffer wrote that interpreting the Bible in a "religious sense" usually means to speak individualistically, and this for him was not at all Christian. He believed very deeply in St. Paul's description of God's presence in Christ as that of a body, the church. In his doctoral dissertation he asserted that the church is "Christ existing as community." Then in his prison correspondence

Bonhoeffer stated his conviction about the social dimension of transcendent experience: "[Jesus'] 'being there for others' is the experience of transcendence . . . not the infinite and unattainable tasks, but the neighbor who is within reach in any given situation" ("Outline for a Book," summer 1944). Since Christian faith is "participation in the being of Jesus," corporate existence is necessary because Jesus is a body, a corpus. To be "in Christ" is to be "in community." Certainly this life in Christ is personal and at times requires solitude, yet the essence of Christian life is to know and experience God together, as the children of God in the family of God. As one can imagine, such an understanding of Christ's corporate nature has deep implications for the sacramental life of the church and of Christian individuals. Just as baptism ought not be seen as a private transaction between God and a person, devoid of the community that gathers and helps nurture each new life in Christ, so holy communion ought never be seen as a private reception of forgiveness apart from the community that bears both the sins of its members and the salvation of its God. While in prison, Bonhoeffer was reminded of the importance of the communal essence of faith by its absence; he daily longed for the physical presence of other brothers or sisters in Christ to feel the presence of God. For him, community in Christ was not something additional or extra, but something inherent and intrinsic for faith itself. The crumbling pillar of individualistic religion must give way to the richness and blessing of life together in Christ.

Pillar #2

Let us return to the letter of April 30, 1944. After asking "Who Christ really is, for us today," as well as pondering the meaning of such fundamentals as church, sermon, and liturgy, Bonhoeffer creatively reflected on the "location" of God for believing people. While God is — and forever will be — stronger than any human (i.e., omnipotent), more pervasive than anything visible (i.e., omnipresent), and wiser than all worldly spirits (i.e., omniscient), God is here described by Bonhoeffer as the one who is "beyond in the midst of life." Whereas a more traditional pillar of Christian faith characterized God as beyond, meaning removed to the world's outer boundaries, this radical envisioning of God's presence amplifies Christ's incarnational involvement in all of life. God is "beyond" in terms of the quality of life and love; God is not "beyond" in a simple sense of distance, geography, or space. Anyone envisioning a god who stays clear and clean of anything soiled or earthy is not referring to the biblical God whose incarnate presence is called Emmanuel/ Jesus. God's otherness and "beyond" are not metaphysical qualities that distance God from sinful humanity, but rather qualities that deepen the mystery of God's involvement and engagement with sinful humanity "in the middle of the village." On May 29, 1944, Bonhoeffer wrote: "We are to find God in what we know, not in what we don't know. . . . God is no stop-gap; he must be recognized at the centre of life, not when we are at the end . . . in life, and not only when death comes; in health and vigor, and not only in suffering; in our activities, and not only in sin." Our second new pillar is to envision God's presence as "beyond in the midst of life." How might such a re-visioning of God's will and work inspire people today?

Pillar #3

As Bonhoeffer thought from prison about the ways that his godson, Dietrich Bethge, might live as a disciple of Jesus Christ, he wrote: "Our being Christians today will be limited to two things: prayer and righteous action among men" (May 1944). Why only "prayer and righteous action"? Has Bonhoeffer here abandoned his loyalty to Barth and Luther and St. Paul with their "theology of the Word"? Is not being Christian also to hear and preach the Word and receive and offer the sacraments? Yes, but one must, according to Bonhoeffer, be careful here — not only courageous — when considering how the Word of God is to be shared with the world. What James Carroll describes as the "incredibility of a church grown drunk with power," Dietrich Bonhoeffer witnessed firsthand in Germany. In the May 1944 sermon for the baptism of his godson, Dietrich Bethge, he wrote:

> Our Church, which has been fighting in these years only for its self-preservation, as though that were an end in itself, is incapable of taking the word of reconciliation and redemption to all men and the world. Our earlier words are therefore bound to lose their force and cease. . . .

He did, however, envision a time when a witness through

proclamation might again be credible and effective. The sermon continued:

> It is not for us to prophesy the day (though the day will come) when people will once more be called so to utter the word of God that the world will be changed and renewed by it. It will be a new language, perhaps quite non-religious, but liberating and redeeming — as was Jesus' language; it will shock people and yet overcome them by its power; it will be the language of a new righteousness and truth. . . . Till then the Christian cause will be a silent and hidden affair, but there will be those who pray and do right and wait for God's own time.

Because words can be superficial and lack an authentic connection to reality, Bonhoeffer cautioned the church against mere verbal proclamation that might make Christ's real presence impossible to know. Incredibility results from words and actions that do not match. The church of Bonhoeffer's day had grown too self-centered and self-serving, such that any proclaimed words about a Christ who reached out to others would necessarily sound unreal, compared with the church's actual deeds. A contemporary example of this gap between words and deeds: "I cannot hear your words because your actions are too loud." It was Bonhoeffer's conviction that mere words or religious practice, devoid of actions to support them, would not be helpful or true. Prayer — words between God and people — joined with "righteous action" would be Christ's manner of existence until a time when words again could truthfully and authentically conform to deeds. He wrote:

> The most important witness of the Christian community before the world is the deed. If the deed becomes a powerful testimony, then the world will inquire about the beliefs that lie behind such a deed.[1]

Our third new pillar regards the manner and means of Christ's presence. Bonhoeffer was here suggesting that Christ's presence in the church for the world will be that of (personal) prayer and (public) action, not one of simple repetition of traditional words, proclamation, and platitudes. To what degree are Christian/church actions today in conflict with their professed and proclaimed beliefs?

Pillar #4

In the letter of July 16, 1944 (quoted earlier), Bonhoeffer very disturbingly, yet constructively, summarized what he understood to be the "decisive difference" between generic religion and Christian faith: "Man's religiosity makes one look in distress to the power of God in the world. . . . The Bible directs man to God's powerlessness and suffering." Two days later, continuing his reflections on what makes Christian discipleship unique, he wrote: "It is not the religious act that makes the Christian, but participation in the sufferings of God in the

---

1. Dietrich Bonhoeffer, *Gesammelte Schriften*, vol. 5 (Munich: Christian Kaiser Verlag, 1972), p. 259.

secular life . . . a person is summoned to share in God's suffering at the hands of a godless world." A fourth new pillar for Bonhoeffer regards the content and meaning of suffering. Here he observed, and then addressed, a common misunderstanding of Christian discipleship. On July 21, 1944, he wrote:

> I'm still discovering right up to this moment, that it is only by living completely in this world that one learns to have faith. . . . By this-worldliness I mean living unreservedly in life's duties, problems, successes and failures, experiences and perplexities. In so doing we throw ourselves completely into the arms of God, taking seriously not our own sufferings, but those of God in the world — watching with Christ in Gethsemane.

One gets the impression that all people (yes, even Christians) naturally see religion as invoking God's power to address one's personal suffering; in contrast, this-worldly, mature Christian spirituality takes more seriously the willingness of people to employ their human power to address the sufferings of God in the world. The poem "Christians and Pagans" (quoted earlier) reflects the same refocusing required of the Christian: Christ's kingdom and God's suffering are to be the focus of Christian discipleship, not the individual person's life, loves, and problems. The challenge then becomes for the disciple of Christ, in a manner reminiscent of the words of John Fitzgerald Kennedy in his inaugural address, to "ask not what God can do for you, but what you can do for God."

One stumbling block to overcome is the rather ancient, persistent, yet not Christian idea that suffering is simply the result of a curse or punishment of God. While biblical tradition teaches that the world's brokenness was not God's design in creation but a result of humankind's rebellion, we have come to know that suffering is larger than any single sin or transgression. Consequently, remaining distant from suffering, on the assumption that God is intentionally absent, may be ancient and persistent — even religious — but not Christian. The disciples of Jesus are called to approach, embrace, and redeem suffering, because God does so, too!

The fourth new pillar, then, is that Christian spirituality is "participation in the powerlessness of God in the world . . . sharing in the suffering of God in Christ" (July 18th). How might one be comforted in suffering by the presence of empathetic persons who come in the name of God?

Pillar #5

A fifth new pillar is authentic maturity of life with God in Christ. In place of the crumbling pillar of immature dependency discussed earlier, Bonhoeffer proposed that the world's coming of age *(die mündig gewordene Welt)* was something to be affirmed and uplifted. In place of the church's critical and condemnatory attitude towards the world's autonomy and growth, there needs to be a recognition and celebration that such advancement and progress is, in fact, God-willed and good. On June 8, 1944, Bonhoeffer referred to

> The movement that began about the 13th century towards the autonomy of man . . . [whereby m]an has learnt to deal with himself in all questions of impor-

tance without recourse to the "working hypothesis" called "God." . . . "God" is being pushed more and more out of life, losing more and more ground. . . . Efforts are made to prove to a world thus come of age that it cannot live without the tutelage of "God."

· Perhaps because of his upbringing in a highly respected family of jurists and scientists, as well as his liberal education at the Kaiser Wilhelm University in early twentieth-century Berlin, Bonhoeffer felt an innate desire to affirm the advancements in learning with all their attendant risks and rewards. In part, because his immediate family was so involved in the cultural renaissance of early twentieth-century Europe, Dietrich Bonhoeffer learned very early in life a deep respect for the contributions of physics, chemistry, history, medicine, law, and psychology, to name only some. He came to see the advancement of knowledge and culture as God-willed, and the traditional criticism of these by the church as not only unnecessary, but quite unchristian. In the June 8 letter he continued:

The attack by Christian apologetic on the adulthood of the world I consider to be in the first place pointless, in the second place ignoble, and in the third place unchristian. Pointless, because it seems to me like an attempt to put a grown-up man back into adolescence, i.e., to make one dependent on things on which one is, in fact, no longer dependent, and thrusting one into problems that are, in fact, no longer problems. Ignoble, because it amounts to an attempt to exploit man's weaknesses for purposes that are alien to him and to which he has not freely assented; unchristian, because it confuses Christ with one particular stage in humanity's religiousness, i.e., with a human law.

The maturity of which Bonhoeffer speaks concerning the world, and therefore the church in the world, is related to his experience of God "in the midst" of the world. The same God who meets people in the "middle of the village" now "takes hold of a person at the centre of life." He summarized in a letter of June 30, 1944, the focus of his reflections: "how to claim for Jesus Christ a world that has come of age."

Later, picking up on his concern, he wrote on July 16: "Now for a few more thoughts on our theme. . . ." It is in this letter that one can be confused and understandably frustrated with Bonhoeffer's reflections. It is here that he foresees possible anxiety in the souls of persons who will conclude that maturity would likely lead to a rejection, displacement, or denial of God. If humans do not "need" God, then some would suppose that God would lose God's place! Many would likely "condemn the whole development that has brought them to such straits." Christian maturity was rather, for Bonhoeffer, a God-willed development, in fact, a very significant point in life when Jesus Christ makes claim on his disciples for prayer and righteous action. No longer would people merely depend on God out of fear, only calling upon God when in dire straits, seeking God's rescue at wits' end. Jesus Christ calls persons to relate to God out of love, to ask God to employ their strengths, to seek direction in helping rescue others. Maturity (*mündigkeit*) is, for Bonhoeffer, the logical/chronological sequel that follows infancy and adolescence; Christians, like all people, are called to responsible living as they mature. Bonhoeffer was suggesting not an immature dependency on God, but a mature interdependency for and with God. And so, he wrote: "God would have us know that we must live as men who manage our lives without him . . . before God and with God we live without God" (July 16th). It is essential that we understand Bonhoeffer's affirmation of worldly and Christian maturity not as a historical point of moral perfection or completion, but as a point of God-willed human development of responsibility in place of adolescent self-centeredness and immaturity. *Mündigkeit* (maturity) refers literally to a person having reached age twenty-one, at which point adult responsible interdependence is expected. It is here that Bonhoeffer's language and thoughts can easily be misunderstood. To not "need" a micromanaging god does not mean one will or should, therefore, reject God. Rather, one is now, more than ever before, able to freely worship and serve God, precisely because it is not demanded! To speak of authentic maturity, for the world and for the Christian, is to affirm what God is bringing to pass with the unfolding of history. "The world that has come of age is more godless, and perhaps for that very reason, nearer to God, than the world before its coming of age" (July 18th). Our fifth new pillar is the posture of authentic maturity that disciples of Christ are to have before God. Is it possible that spiritual maturity is what people not only need but ultimately want?

As we near the end of the summer of 1944, the somewhat fragmentary reflections of Bonhoeffer do suggest an answer to his central life question, first asked in the April 30th "theological letter": "Who Christ really is, for us today." In his "Outline for a Book," Bonhoeffer began to sketch what he hoped would later be his contribution to church and theology. The book would have three chapters: "A Stocktaking of Christianity"; "The Real Meaning of Christian Faith"; "Conclusions." Faith is "participation in the being of Jesus (incarnation, cross, and resurrection)"; the church is made up of those who "exist for others." As Eberhard Bethge later wrote, "Bonhoeffer added a new title to the old ones of Jesus, one that is both intelligible and at the same time profound: 'the man for others.'"[2] Bonhoeffer's observation was that the church often appeared self-serving and ingrown. To "exist for others" naturally entailed involvement in the midst of the secular world, not escape from it; further, maturity would be exhibited as co-responsibility for God's world, rather than adolescent dependence, denial, or detachment. In his doctoral dissertation in 1927 he wrote: "This being-with-each-other of the church community and its members through Christ already entails their being-for-each-other. . . . Christ died for the church community so that it may live one life, with each other and for each other."[3]

Are Bonhoeffer's observations and proposals realistic? Were these only the ramblings of a person under great stress who tried to redesign the church and re-envision the world to make sense of his crumbling world? It remains up to us,

2. Eberhard Bethge, *Dietrich Bonhoeffer — Man of Vision, Man of Courage* (New York: Harper and Row, 1970), p. 790.

3. Dietrich Bonhoeffer, *Sanctorum Communio* (Minneapolis: Fortress Press, 1998), pp. 182, 184.

those who follow these many years later, to consider if and how the pillars Bonhoeffer proposed are truthful and helpful in our time. I think they may be.

CHAPTER IV

The Pillars Outside of the Prison (Writings)

W hile the intent of this book is to make the prison reflections of Dietrich Bonhoeffer more accessible and
influential for the church of our day, it is also helpful to describe, even briefly, something of his earlier writings because
there exists a deep sense of continuity between 1927 and 1944.
We discover in Bonhoeffer's doctoral dissertation, *The Communion of Saints* (1927), through the *Christology* lectures of 1933,
to the outline for Christian community in *Life Together,* and
woven into the chapters of *Discipleship* and *Ethics* (to mention
only the more well-known titles), important insights and
themes that appear later in *Letters and Papers from Prison.* Although shifts of emphasis result from changed life circumstances within those years, this sense of continuity is evident
as Bonhoeffer labored to dynamically experience — and then
express — the reality of Christ's presence.

With the recently completed seventeen-volume critical
edition *Dietrich Bonhoeffer Werke* (Munich: Christian Kaiser
Verlag) and the upcoming English edition titled *Dietrich
Bonhoeffer Works* (Minneapolis: Fortress Press), the texts and
the contexts for the extant writings of Bonhoeffer are solidly
in place and available for anyone seriously interested. The

following references are only to provide glimpses of his earlier insights.

At the relatively young age of twenty-one, Dietrich Bonhoeffer had completed the requirements for a doctoral degree in theology at Berlin's Kaiser Wilhelm University, including a dissertation titled *Sanctorum Communio*. Not something that received much notice immediately, *The Communion of Saints* was later described by Karl Barth as a "theological miracle." Using the tools and language of sociology and theology, Bonhoeffer argued that the unique nature of the church results from its being divine and human, much as Jesus himself was. This incarnational approach to faith and theology would later support and sustain his convictions relating to "Christ existing as community," as well as experiencing Christ "in the middle of the village."

In the foreword to *The Communion of Saints* (New York: Harper and Row) Eberhard Bethge wrote in 1960 when republishing *Sanctorum Communio:*

> The student of Bonhoeffer who wishes to know the sources of his "religionless interpretation of Biblical Concepts in a world come of age," the worldly Christianity of the letters from prison, will have to turn to Bonhoeffer's earlier writings. There he will find both the basis and the starting-point for the ideas in the letters.

As a doctoral dissertation, *Sanctorum Communio* was not intended for general public consumption. His preface offers a glimpse of the subject matter.

This study places social philosophy and sociology in the service of dogmatics . . . the subject matter under discussion belongs to dogmatics, not to the sociology of religion. The inquiry into Christian social philosophy and sociology is a genuinely dogmatic one, since it can be answered only if our starting point is the concept of the Church.

Dietrich Bonhoeffer followed up his academic training in theology by spending a year in Barcelona, Spain, as a vicar in a German-speaking congregation. During this year (1927-28) he was experiencing congregational life while contemplating whether his future should include the (academic) podium or the (congregational) pulpit. He chose to return to Berlin the following year as a *Privatdozent* (entry-level instructor), beginning then to lecture in his chosen field of theology. First he had to fulfill a requirement by delivering a *Habilitationschrift,* which for him was *Akt und Sein (Act and Being).* This exercise in philosophical/theological reflection qualified him to teach on the theological faculty.

Shortly into his appointment to the faculty of perhaps Germany's most prestigious university, Bonhoeffer seized the opportunity to spend one year as a Sloan Fellow at New York City's Union Theological Seminary. This year of postgraduate study allowed him not only to study under persons like Reinhold Niebuhr, but also to experience the preaching of William Sloan Coffin at Riverside Church, share in teaching Sunday School at Harlem's Abyssinian Baptist Church, and feel the pulse of America's urban poor during the Great Depression. He would later describe the importance of this year for his life maturation, yet at the time, he thought mainline American church life somewhat innocuous and American theology superficial and clearly inferior to its European counterpart. Bonhoeffer's most life-changing experiences while in America were the occasions he spent relating to black Americans in Harlem. There he thought the presence of God — in suffering and hope — was authentically experienced.

In the fall of 1931 Bonhoeffer's full-time teaching career began in Berlin, where he also taught confirmation and served as a chaplain at the Technical University of Berlin. First published in English as *Christ the Center* (New York: Harper and Row, 1966), his lectures on Christology during the summer of 1933 provide us with a glimpse of the theological foundation that would ground him until his dying day. In solid academic fashion, these lectures began by tracing some of the history of christological reflection, moving naturally, yet quite radically, to his own formulations for understanding the content and meaning of Christian faith: Jesus Christ himself. The same Christ who in Bonhoeffer's 1944 prison reflections was known as the "beyond in the midst of life" is described in the christological lectures of 1933 as "at the center of human existence, history and nature." In the prison reflections, the same Christ who through Christians "participates in the sufferings of God in the world" can be seen eleven years earlier in Bonhoeffer's christological lectures: "In the humiliation, Christ enters the world of sin and death of his own free will. He enters in such a way as to hide in it in weakness and not to be known as God-man."[1] Edwin Robertson

---

1. Dietrich Bonhoeffer, *Christ the Center* (New York: Harper and Row, 1966), p. 111.

wrote in the Introduction to the English edition of the christo-logical lectures:

> Our principal danger today is that we shall only use those writings that came out of the experience of his [Bonhoeffer's] last days. This would be an injustice to one of the greatest theologians of our time. The [christological] lectures . . . are necessary as a basis for understanding what Bonhoeffer was hinting at in the occasional papers from prison. We need both the early framework of his thinking and the brilliant insights that he himself attempts to interpret within this framework. The two together give us the voice of the prophet.[2]

One of the most difficult parts of Bonhoeffer's two-year imprisonment (setting aside the anxiety from the uncertainty of a date for his trial and the stress created by the necessity for deception and cover-up) was the isolation from his friends and family. Although weekly visits from close family provided something he looked forward to and from which he savored rich memories, the earlier fellowship known in the Confessing Church Seminary at Finkenwalde — and later within the Brethren House and Collective Pastorate — was deeply missed. Often in prison he would share how the closeness of community, as described in *Life Together,* was what he missed most. There is good reason why this brief book has been widely read and broadly acclaimed; it was written to describe

2. Dietrich Bonhoeffer, *Christ the Center* (New York: Harper and Row, 1966), p. 23.

the structure and dynamics of communal life that he established at a *Predigerseminar* (preacher's seminary) for his seminarians who were preparing for ministry in the anti-Nazi Confessing Church between 1935 and 1937. The popularity of *Life Together* across denominational lines would suggest its contents are not so much the controversial "new pillars" being suggested by Bonhoeffer, but rather traditional, yet obviously relevant, anchors for faith and life. In a similar vein, *Discipleship* (first printed in English as *The Cost of Discipleship* and in German, *Nachfolge*) has enjoyed a perennial appeal by an even more diverse audience. Perhaps the most well known of anything he wrote, *Discipleship* offers insights and challenges about living out Christian faith in a direct and more prescriptive manner. Different personalities seem to laud, or languish over, this Christian classic for the same reasons: positively, it offers concrete guidance for life in Christ; negatively, for some, it offers (too much) concrete guidance and seems legalistic.

One of Bonhoeffer's life regrets was that he had not completed his work on Christian ethics. After his death and the end of the Second World War, Eberhard Bethge assembled the fragments of Bonhoeffer's cumulative attempts to write *Ethics* (New York: Macmillan, 1955). While the exact ordering and dating of the parts has been debated to the present day, there is no question that an organic unity exists between the formal ethics materials and Bonhoeffer's more informal prison reflections. One would expect such (relatively) coterminous writings to bear a resemblance; this organic unity confirms and reinforces the view that his prison reflections were not aberrations but concepts consistent with, and intrinsic to, his entire life. Especially the sections "The Total and Exclusive Claim of Christ," "Guilt,

Justification and Renewal," "Christ, Reality and Good," and "What Is Meant by Telling the Truth" can be read proleptically into the prison writings. While clearly more challenging because of its academic intent, *Ethics* will always remain a significant part of the Bonhoeffer legacy, and will hold an important place in the history of Christian ethics.

There is little question that the writings of Bonhoeffer described above will continue to inspire scholars and laity well into the future. Hopefully, the lesser-known occasional papers, lectures, sermons, and letters will also remain in circulation. Bonhoeffer scholars Geffrey B. Kelly and F. Burton Nelson authored *A Testament to Freedom: The Essential Writings of Dietrich Bonhoeffer* (San Francisco: HarperSanFrancisco, 1990) in the hopes of providing the general public with a selection of materials, beyond just the most well known. Earlier, Edwin Robertson edited three volumes of collected works that provided the English-speaking world with a variety of Bonhoeffer materials; *No Rusty Swords, The Way to Freedom,* and *True Patriotism* (New York: Harper and Row, 1965, 1966, 1973, respectively) present selections from the German six-volume *Gesammelte Schriften* (Munich: Christian Kaiser Verlag, 1965-74). The appendices in the back of this book list the primary (and some selected secondary) English-language sources of the Bonhoeffer legacy. His is a legacy that resembles human personality; one can enjoy a relationship on several levels, yet greater fascination and mystery continue to surface the deeper one digs, the more open one is, the longer one looks. A goal of this small book is "to make more accessible" the profound yet practical, the constructive and the critical insights of this twentieth-century Christian disciple and martyr.

CHAPTER V

The Discipline Needed to Know
When the Pillars Need Replacement

Dietrich Bonhoeffer's life question, "Who Christ really is
for us today," is really — not just rhetorically — a question. A question can be understood as something merely interim, existing only until an answer is found; when the answer is found, the question is no longer relevant. Not so in
this case, as Bonhoeffer inquires about God's presence, in
Christ, for his own time and place. The question, "Who
Christ really is for us today," is not a problem to be solved,
nor simply an obstacle to be overcome. The concern for him
is a relationship that continually begs for deeper knowledge
and greater commitment.

Second, Bonhoeffer's life question presupposes a history, a past. He knew a considerable amount about Jesus
from the New Testament, Christ in the ancient creeds, the
God proclaimed in preaching and shared in the church's
sacraments. He was not essentially asking an entry-level
question about the person at the center of the church's
proclamation. Bonhoeffer was asking a living question, because the One he was inquiring about was and is living. In
every generation, including Bonhoeffer's, there are gravely
different answers to this living question about God's na-

ture and purpose, all parties ironically appealing to similar histories.

Bonhoeffer observed, while visiting the epileptic hospital in Bethel in 1933, that God's person and presence were experienced there protecting the handicapped and guarding the vulnerable persons then marginalized by society. He had great admiration for its director, Friedrich von Bodelschwingh, whose respect for the sacredness of all life was very evident. At this same time, Bonhoeffer observed Nazi doctors who believed, and then acted on their beliefs, that God's presence endorsed euthanizing those same handicapped persons, who were deemed "unworthy of life." Which belief, which God was true? Bonhoeffer's life and death witness to God's solidarity with the vulnerable, the weak, the persecuted, the rejected, the downtrodden. While theologically desiring that Jews come "to know God through the grace and mercy of Jesus Christ," Dietrich Bonhoeffer consistently defended every human being as a creation of God, especially offering help to those who could not defend themselves. This mission of solidarity and defense he understood to be the work of Jesus himself.

Bonhoeffer was one of the persons responsible for inspiring the formation of the Confessing Church (*Bekennende Kirche*) in 1934, created to oppose the heretical preaching and teaching of the movement that called itself "Deutsche Christen" (German Christians), which fully supported the plans of the Hitler government and became more and more powerful in the life and work of Germany's established state church. Again, he interpreted the actions of the Nazis not merely politically or sociologically, but theologically.

Bonhoeffer's criticism of German Christian theology was deeply christological; he believed early on that the German Christian "answer" to the question, "Who Christ really is for us today," was gravely wrong and amounted to a German domestication of the Christ of biblical tradition and the Lord of the Christian church. Yet, scores of Germans answered this question in conformity with the Reich bishop and the prevailing winds of German Christendom at that time. Hindsight is remarkably accurate and significantly more "predictable" than foresight. As we look back on Bonhoeffer's "answer" to the question "Who Christ really is for us today" (namely, the incarnate God-man who lived and died inviting all human beings into relationship with God), it seems so obvious that all other answers (e.g., "Christ has come to us in Adolf Hitler" or "Christ's redeeming work is meant for only Aryans") are not real answers at all. Yet, that was not so obvious for many sincere, knowledgeable, Christian people in Europe in 1933. Apparently, the historical/biblical Jesus was not recognized for who he really is. What broke down? How did the traditional answers and confessions of the church fail to defend the world from an anti-Christ? The thousand-year Third Reich of Adolf Hitler was seen to be God's rule, God's presence, God's kingdom. It was one answer to Bonhoeffer's question, but obviously not *his* answer.

And so, every generation of Christians is charged to ask this question, "Who Christ really is for us today." With the wisdom of hindsight and the courage of foresight, we each inquire about Jesus Christ.

Dietrich Bonhoeffer understood very well how the

powers of evil in this world could distort and destroy the presence of God, in Christ, and how even the church and its members (perhaps especially the church and its members) could take part in that distortion and destruction. He watched the Confessing Church erode into distortion, underestimating the real threat of Germany's diabolic, racist leadership. It was in the awareness of the fragileness of God's presence, in Christ, in the world that Bonhoeffer inquired about the need for a "discipline of the secret," a manner of protecting the precious, yet vulnerable Christ, whose presence is in some ways not apparent to the world. Never did Bonhoeffer presume to fully understand or faultlessly practice such discipline; his "life question" is a reminder that the practice of discipline never ends. One could conclude that the static, traditional, institutionalized, domesticated, crumbling pillars of Christianity represented a strait-jacket in which the living God, in Christ, could not budge. The new pillars Bonhoeffer proposed were an attempt to make space for the living God, in Christ, to move "in the middle of the village" to redeem and reconcile. Interestingly, but not surprisingly, Bonhoeffer asked on April 30, 1944, "Does the secret discipline . . . take on new importance here?" And then five days later he wrote: "A secret discipline must be restored whereby the mysteries of the Christian faith are protected against profanation." While these are the most explicit places he speaks of the necessity of discipline for authentic discipleship, he had thought of such a need before. In *Discipleship* (1937) he wrote:

> What happened to the insights of the ancient church,
> which in the baptismal teaching watched so carefully
> over the boundary between the church and the world?[1]

As part of a lecture in the same year to the ordinands at
Finkenwalde he stated: "The Arkandisziplin also began . . . to
provide protection for the Church against the mockery of the
world."[2]

In the early church, the *catechumenate* was a program insti-
tuted to initiate persons into the Christian faith; in a guided
fashion, the baptismal candidates (usually adults) were only
gradually trusted with the sacred realities of faith, so that the
Christ who was present in Word and sacraments would not be
profaned. Most specifically, this preparation before Christian
baptism was to ensure that persons: 1) Understood the price of
becoming a Christian, which would likely involve persecution
at the hands of the pagans; 2) Learned to distinguish Christian
faith from heretical Gnostic beliefs; and 3) Were taught to know
that, because being Christian was now (following Constantine
and Theodosius' edicts of toleration and endorsement) acceptable, it would take more discernment and courage to stand in
faith with Jesus Christ than before. Dietrich Bonhoeffer reflected on this ancient church practice *(disciplina arcani)* because
similar threats were on the horizon for European Christians.

First, the brutality of the SA, SS, and Gestapo in Nazi Germany was not that different from the overt pagan hostility of

1. Dietrich Bonhoeffer, *Discipleship* (Minneapolis: Fortress Press, 2001),
p. 54.
2. Clyde Fant, *Bonhoeffer: Worldly Preaching* (Nashville: Thomas Nelson,
1975), p. 125.

Caracalla (211-217 CE), Maximinus (235-238 CE), Decius (250-251 CE), Gallus (251-252 CE), Valerian (257-258 CE), or Diocletian (303-304 CE), to name only some. Christians, with others, were victims of hate and prejudice. Discipline was needed to help Christians understand and then endure such persecutions.

Second, the heretical distortion by the German Christians, in which the universal intent of the gospel was being replaced with a faith program "designed" only for superior Aryans, was not unlike the heresy of the Gnostic Christians who understood the gospel to be the possession of only the enlightened/superior spiritual ones who received special knowledge from above. Bonhoeffer also knew that the German Christians' belief in a "second" source of divine revelation (i.e., Adolf Hitler) was a direct assault and blasphemous affront to the single Christian source of divine revelation, Jesus Christ. Related to this heretical appeal to an ultimate truth outside of God's revelation in Jesus Christ was the obvious conflict with the Protestant Reformation's commitment to *sola scriptura,* a commitment also close to the hearts of Bonhoeffer, Barth, and the framers of the 1934 Barmen Declaration. So how would Christians remain faithful and true in their worship? Discipline.

Third, the innocuous state of "civic religion," which essentially equated *Christentum* (Christianity) with *Deutschtum* (Germanity), caused Bonhoeffer to reflect on the religious banality that existed following the Constantinian and Theodosian declarations making Christianity first "tolerable" and then the "official" religion of the empire back in 313 CE and 380 CE. Again, discipline would be needed to avoid domestication and distortion of the gospel.

Unfortunately, an uncritical usage of this concept — *disciplina arcani* — has led to a misunderstanding of its meaning and value. Bonhoeffer made use of the term, then employed by church historians of his day, *arkandisziplin;* when Bonhoeffer's prison writings were published in English (*Letters and Papers from Prison*), the translator rendered *arkandisziplin* as "secret discipline," which fails to capture the essential meaning — "discipline of the secret" — from the original Latin, *disciplina arcani.* Until quite recently, it was understood that Bonhoeffer's desire here was for a more private, personal, inward, spiritual practice of faith to complement the more public, communal, outward deeds of justice. More than a translation choice is at stake here. The concept actually means a "discipline of the secret," not a "secret form of religious discipline." My own rendering of this term is "responsible sharing of the mystery of Christian faith." In fact, Bonhoeffer's intent was to reinstate a careful discipline for authentic discipleship in every realm of life, private and public, personal and communal, inward and outward, spiritual and physical. Therefore, *disciplina arcani* was recalled in those 1944 prison letters because Dietrich Bonhoeffer thought that the church then, as in the first centuries, was at risk of losing sight of the love and life of God for all people — in Christ — through Nazi pagan hostility, Aryan theological distortion, and German cultural domestication. And, while Nazi Germany remains a dramatic example of threat to the gospel, God's "secret," the presence of God in the world in Christ, needs witness and disciplined protection in every generation and in every place.

Essentially, a "discipline of the secret" is necessary to preserve and proclaim the dynamic presence of Jesus Christ in a blessed, yet broken, world, in which the disciples of Jesus are called to share in the sufferings of God. The "pillars that crumble" are really static expressions of faith and practice from one time that need refinement or replacement in a new time. The Reformation of the sixteenth century, like the Second Vatican Council of the twentieth century, was an exercise in *disciplina arcani,* "responsible sharing of the mystery of Christian faith." These significant events challenged the static, crumbling pillars of tradition with the dynamic new pillars of Christ's presence.

Epilogue

Dietrich Bonhoeffer is one who sought to experience and express the present reality of God — in Jesus Christ — within a rapidly changing world and a less-than-rapidly changing church. While standing on a solid Christian foundation, Bonhoeffer identified traditional pillars of faith that were crumbling, while simultaneously proposing newer, more dynamic pillars for Christian life, which would bear more authentic witness to the living presence of God. Dietrich Bonhoeffer's life ended on a scaffold in Flossenbürg on April 9, 1945; his wisdom and witness continue to live as *disciplina arcani* ("responsible sharing of the mystery of Christian faith") is practiced in the world by the disciples of Jesus Christ. The circumstances and challenges of life are constantly changing, yet the practice of *disciplina arcani,* on the solid foundation of God's presence, empowers the disciples of Jesus Christ to live and love authentically and faithfully. The church in every age will look different as pillars crumble and then are rebuilt. However, such death and resurrection is built into the very life of God in the world. While it may seem more safe and secure to buttress crumbling pillars of former days, any such restoration fails to understand the dynamic activity of God, who in Jesus Christ calls people to "follow after" *(nachfolgen)* the living God, who in Christ dies and rises every day.

What might *disciplina arcani* suggest for a church desiring to "follow after" Jesus Christ at the beginning of the third millennium CE? What insights of Dietrich Bonhoeffer, discovered in the crucible of Nazi Germany, might assist the church today in more faithfully being "Christ for others"? Our prayers today might well be Bonhoeffer's prayers, when he wrote: "May God in his mercy lead us through these times; but above all, may he lead us to himself" (July 21, 1944), and ". . . boldly we'll face the future, come what may. At even and morn God will befriend us . . ." (December 1944).

One traditional pillar of the church that Bonhoeffer identified as crumbling, yet still today — perhaps especially today — remains attractive and persistent, is that of individualistic religion. For a variety of reasons, the details of which lie outside the scope of this book, much Christian proclamation and programming is focused on faith in a god that offers primarily personal meaning and fulfillment. Marketing the faith therefore amounts to showing the consumer what is offered and how the product (the faith) benefits the buyer. Yes, even religion can become a product to be marketed and sold; *disciplina arcani* can assist the church in proclaiming a message and a Messiah who calls disciples to a "life for others." This difference of emphasis or focus is no small matter! Contemporary forms of individualistic religion or spirituality have become very attractive and, while they are in some sense "religious," are not at all faithful to the call of Jesus Christ to be a "church for others." While Christian discipleship certainly results in personal fulfillment and deeper life meaning, such fulfillment and meaning are always a result, not a goal, of loving one's neighbor, serving others. Bonhoeffer's insight here seems as relevant today as it was a half century ago.

A second traditional pillar of the church that Bonhoeffer identified as crumbling, yet still today remains attractive and persistent, is that of an emphasis or focus in religion on "otherworldliness." There has always been, and will likely always be, religious preoccupation for many people in things beyond death and outside the realm of history. Apocalypticism continues to spread its unhistorical, unchristian, and unhealthy seeds among people quite willing to water such seeds. At the turn of the third millennium the book/film series *Left Behind* was catapulted into a best-selling status. Authors Tim LaHaye and Jerry Jenkins created fictitious scenarios combining "historical/factual" biblical imagery with fictional characters of the present to promote their unhistorical, unchristian, unhealthy apocalypticism. For sure, the deceptive combination of "biblical fact" and contemporary fiction, by which the authors seduce and scare their readers, is unethical. *Disciplina arcani* could assist the church today to more clearly experience God as "beyond in our midst." Life here and now is, at times, overwhelming and frightening. A fascination with fear and the unknown, combined with a promise of release from this world's pain and discomfort for those somehow privileged to escape, is what has made the *Left Behind* series attractive to many people. Yet, God's call, and the commission for the disciples of Jesus, is to live and love the world that God made, here and now. Certain brands of religion encourage apocalyptic escapism from the world.

Disciplina arcani fosters unselfish loving engagement in the world, as Jesus lived and died.

A third traditional pillar of the church that Bonhoeffer identified as crumbling, yet still today remains attractive and persistent is that of uncritical verbal proclamation and evangelism. Observing that traditional theological words and concepts, even though still meaningful to some religious people, had become inauthentic and hypocritical to those outside the church, Bonhoeffer stressed the need for loving deeds in public, supported by Christian prayers in private. Today, one can also see proclamation and evangelism that contradicts the dynamic presence of God, in Christ, because of hypocritical deeds. *Disciplina arcani* challenges the church, and all disciples of Christ, to constantly weigh their words against their deeds. When, and if, words render Christ's presence incredible, the disciples' loving deeds and personal prayers continue, while verbal/public expression waits for a more appropriate time.

A fourth traditional pillar of the church that Dietrich Bonhoeffer identified as crumbling yet still remains attractive and persistent is the idea that equates earthly blessing with the presence of God and earthly suffering with the absence of God. This traditional religious assumption regarding blessing and curse from God was challenged in Jesus Christ, discussed in the life of a person like Job, and readdressed in lives like Bonhoeffer. While faced with disproportionate suffering and undeserved pain, the victims of Nazi brutality occasioned for Dietrich Bonhoeffer a questioning of God's ways and a theology of God's suffering. He came to understand that God participates in human suffering, not that God causes human suffering. Further, as God suffers in the pain of humanity, so are God's servants to share in the pain of humanity. Christian discipleship means addressing, not avoiding the pains of people. Bonhoeffer left the ultimate mystery of suffering (theodicy) with God and the response to suffering with people.

A particular challenge in the age of instant communication is information overload. As never before, people can overdose on images of suffering as horrific global pain constantly bombards daily lives. With massive suffering seen everywhere everyday, *disciplina arcani* will be necessary to proclaim that Jesus Christ accompanies individuals and communities as they address the suffering within reach, rather than be paralyzed by volumes of suffering that can never be addressed. *Disciplina arcani* assists the disciples of Jesus engage and share in suffering (the world's and therefore God's), rather than treat it as God's curse or absence and then labor to avoid it.

A fifth and final traditional pillar of the church that Dietrich Bonhoeffer identified as crumbling, yet still remains attractive and persistent, is that of religious immaturity, that is, childish dependence on God. It has perhaps always been a temptation for religious persons to seek sanctuary in the arms of the Almighty when threatened by storms without and enemies within. Without losing an ultimate sense of security, the disciples of Christ are to maturely engage and responsibly manage the world God created. *Disciplina arcani* reminds the church and her people that Jesus Christ is dynamically involved in the contemporary issues of creation and culture. Maturity *(mündigkeit)* for Bonhoeffer requires that people address life issues, such as genetic engineering, cloning, amniocentesis, and nuclear energy, as well as face challenges like global warming, ozone depletion, and limited fossil fuels. Desiring a simpler past, or hankering for a more pastoral future, may seem in some sense religious, but God — in Jesus Christ — challenges persons to "boldly face the future, come what may" ("Powers of Good," December 1944). God's will for humanity is still to have dominion (Genesis 1 and 2), and responsible dominion requires maturity, not childish dependence.

In fact, the words and witness of Dietrich Bonhoeffer provide much wisdom for the church beginning the third millennium CE as it strives to faithfully live in the presence of Jesus Christ. In a world and church that is often individualistic, the call of Jesus Christ is to be "people for others"; in a world and church desiring God in "otherworldliness," the call of Jesus Christ is to know God's "beyond in the midst" of life; in a world and a church that risks incredibility as its words and deeds conflict, the call of Jesus Christ is to refrain from religious rhetoric and simply love one's neighbor, until a later, appropriate time for words arrives.

The primary confession of the Christian community before the world is the deed, which interprets itself. When the deed becomes a powerful thing, then the world will inquire about the verbal confession behind such deeds.[1]

1. Dietrich Bonhoeffer, *Gesammelte Schriften,* vol. 5, p. 259, translation mine.

In a world and church where pain and suffering are seen as God's curse or absence, the disciples of Jesus Christ are called to live in solidarity with those who suffer, in the knowledge that God's suffers (*theopathy*) and calls people to share in God's suffering; in a world and church where fear of God and anxiety for the future cause people to assume a posture of immature dependence before the Almighty, Jesus Christ calls disciples to trust the love of God and accept the role of stewarding the world with God in a mature and interdependent manner.

I trust it has become clear just how Christ-centered the spirituality of Dietrich Bonhoeffer really is. Contrary to notions that Bonhoeffer lost his Christian faith in prison, it seems evident that his reflections, when understood and in context, reveal an ever deeper faith and walk with Jesus Christ. On a solid Christian foundation Bonhoeffer proposed new, dynamic pillars that would make the church faithful and relevant in his day. Hopefully, it is clear just how relevant his insights are for our day as well.

"Anxious souls will ask" whenever radical questions appear to undermine or destroy cherished pillars of faith, inherited from the past. Yet, trust in the faithfulness of God, who has established a solid foundation, can allow and encourage the building of newer, relevant pillars of faith in every generation, as we seek to authentically "follow after" Jesus Christ.

Selections from Dietrich Bonhoeffer's Letters and Papers from Prison

April 30, 1944

"You would be surprised, and perhaps even worried, by my theological thoughts and the conclusions that they lead to.... What is bothering me incessantly is the question what Christianity really is, or indeed who Christ really is, for us today.... We are moving toward a completely religionless time; ... what does that mean for 'Christianity'? ... The questions to be answered would surely be: What do a church, a community, a sermon, a liturgy, a Christian life mean in a religionless world? ... People as they are now simply cannot be religious any more. How do we speak in a 'secular' way about 'God'? What is the meaning of worship and prayer in a religionless situation? Does the 'discipline of the secret' ... take on new importance here? ... Religious people speak of God when human knowledge ... has come to an end, or when human resources fail.... I should like to speak of God not on the boundaries but at the centre, not in weakness but in strength; and therefore not in death and guilt but in man's life and goodness.... God is beyond in the midst of our life. The church stands, not at the boundaries where human powers give out, but in the middle of the village. . . . How this . . . looks, what form it takes, is something that I'm thinking about a great deal."

May 5, 1944
"What does it mean to 'interpret in a religious sense'? I think it means to speak on the one hand metaphysically, and on the other hand individualistically. Neither of these is relevant to the Biblical message or to the man of today."

Thoughts on the Day of the Baptism of Dietrich Wilhelm Rüdiger Bethge
May 1944
"Our church, which has been fighting in these years only for its self-preservation, as though that were an end in itself, is incapable of taking the word of reconciliation and redemption to mankind and the world. Our earlier words are therefore bound to lose their force and cease, and our being Christians today will be limited to two things: prayer and righteous action among men. It is not for us to prophesy the day (though the day will come) when men will once more be called so to utter the word of God that the world will be changed and renewed by it. It will be a new language, perhaps quite nonreligious, but liberating and redeeming — as was Jesus' language; it will shock people and yet overcome them by its power; it will be the language of a new righteousness and truth, proclaiming God's peace with men and the coming of

his kingdom. . . . Till then the Christian cause will be a silent and hidden affair, but there will be those who pray and do right and wait for God's own time."

May 29, 1944

"We are to find God in what we know, not in what we don't know; God wants us to realize his presence, not in unsolved problems but in those that are solved. That is true of the relationship between God and scientific knowledge, but it is also true of the wider human problems of death, suffering, and guilt. . . . Here again, God is no stop-gap; he must be recognized at the centre of life, not when we are at the end of our resources; it is his will to be recognized in life, and not only when death comes; in health and vigour, and not only in suffering; in our activities, and not only in sin."

June 8, 1944

"The movement that began about the thirteenth century . . . towards the autonomy of man . . . [whereby] man has learnt to deal with himself in all questions of importance without recourse to the 'working hypothesis' called 'God.' . . . 'God' is being pushed more and more out of life, losing more and more ground. . . . The world that has become conscious of itself and the laws that govern its own existence has grown self-confident. . . . Christian apologetic has taken the most varied forms of opposition to this self-assurance. Efforts are made to prove to a world come of age that it cannot live without the tutelage of 'God.' Even though there has been surrender on all secular problems, there still remains the so-called 'ultimate questions' — death, guilt — to which only 'God' can give an answer, and because of which we need God and the church and the pastor. . . . But what if one day they [these questions] no longer exist as such, if they too can be answered 'without God'? . . . The attack by Christian apologetic on the adulthood of the world I consider to be in the first place pointless, in the second place ignoble, and in the third place unchristian. Pointless, because it seems to be like an attempt to put a grown-up man back into adolescence, i.e. to make him dependent on things on which he is, in fact, no longer dependent, and thrusting him into problems that are, in fact, no longer problems to him. Ignoble, because it amounts to an attempt to exploit man's weakness for purposes that are alien to him and to which he has not freely assented. Unchristian, because it confuses Christ with one particular stage in man's religiousness. . . . The question is: Christ and the world that has come of age."

June 27, 1944
"The Christian, unlike the devotees of the redemption myths, has no last line of escape available from earthly tasks and difficulties into the eternal, but, like Christ himself . . . , he just drinks the earthly cup to the dregs, and only in his doing so is the crucified and risen Lord with him, and he crucified and risen with Christ. . . . Christ takes hold of a man at the centre of his life."

July 16, 1944
"Anxious souls will ask what room there is now left for God. . . . And we cannot be honest unless we recognize that we have to live in the world *etsi deus non daretur*. And this is just

what we do recognize — before God! ... God would have us know that we must live as men who manage our lives without him. The God who is with us is the God who forsakes us (Mark 15:34). The God who lets us live in the world without the working hypothesis of God is the God before whom we stand continually. Before God and with God we live without God. God lets himself be pushed out of the world onto the cross. He is weak and powerless in the world, and that is precisely the way, the only way, in which he is with us and helps us. ... Here is the decisive difference between Christianity and all religions. Man's religiosity makes him look in his distress to the power of God in the world: God is the *deus ex machina*. The Bible directs man to God's powerlessness and suffering; only the suffering God can help."

July 18, 1944

"The poem about Christians and pagans contains an idea that you will recognize: 'Christians stand by God in his hour of grieving'; that is what distinguishes Christians from pagans.... Man is summoned to share in God's sufferings at the hands of a godless world. ... It is not the religious act that makes the Christian, but participation in the sufferings of God in the secular life ... not in the first place thinking about one's own needs, problems, sins, and fears, but allowing oneself to be caught up into the way of Jesus Christ.... But what does this life look like, this participation in the powerlessness of God in the world? ... The world that has come of age is more godless, and perhaps for that very reason nearer to God, than the world before its coming of age. Forgive me for still putting it all so terribly clumsily and badly, as I really feel I am."

July 21, 1944

"I'm still discovering right up to this moment, that it is only by living completely in this world that one learns to have faith. . . . By this-worldliness I mean living unreservedly in life's duties, problems, successes and failures, experiences and perplexities. In so doing we throw ourselves completely into the arms of God, taking seriously, not our own sufferings, but those of God in the world — watching with Christ in Gethsemane . . . that is how one becomes a man and a Christian (cf. Jer. 45!). . . . How can success make us arrogant, or failure lead us astray, when we share in God's sufferings through a life of this kind? . . . May God in his mercy lead us through these times; but above all, may he lead us to himself."

Outline for a Book — Summer 1944

". . . a transformation of all human life is given in the fact that 'Jesus is there only for others'. His 'being there for others' is the experience of transcendence. . . . Faith is participation in this being of Jesus (incarnation, cross, and resurrection). . . . The transcendental is not infinite and unattainable tasks, but the neighbor who is within reach in any given situation. . . . The church is the church only when it exists for others. . . . The church must share in the secular problems of ordinary human life, not dominating, but helping and serving."

Writings of Dietrich Bonhoeffer

(Listed below are the dates of writing, the English titles, and the original publishers/dates.)

(1930)
The Communion of Saints. New York: Harper and Row, 1963.

(1931)
Act and Being. New York: Harper and Row, 1961 (reprinted by Octagon Books, 1983).

(1933)
Creation and Fall: A Theological Interpretation of Genesis 1–3. New York: Macmillan, 1959.

(1933)
Christ the Center. New York: Harper and Row, 1966, 1978.

(1935-39)
Spiritual Care. Translated by Jay C. Rochelle. Philadelphia: Fortress Press, 1985.

(1937)
The Cost of Discipleship. New York: Macmillan, 1949, 1960, 1963.

(1938)
Temptation. New York: Macmillan, 1955.

(1939)
Life Together. New York: Harper and Row, 1954.

(1940)
Psalms: The Prayer Book of the Bible. Minneapolis: Augsburg, 1970.

(1940-43)
Ethics. New York: Macmillan, 1955, 1965.

(1943)
Fiction from Prison: Gathering Up the Past. Philadelphia: Fortress, 1981.

(1943-44)
Letters and Papers from Prison. London: SCM, 1953, 1967, 1971.

(1928-36)
No Rusty Swords. New York: Harper and Row, 1965.

(1935-39)
The Way to Freedom. New York: Harper and Row, 1966.

(1939-45)
True Patriotism. New York: Harper and Row, 1973.

(1941-44)
I Loved This People. Richmond, Va.: John Knox Press, 1965.

Gesammelte Schriften. Edited by Eberhard Bethge. Munich: Christian Kaiser Verlag, 1965-74.

Meditating on the Word. Edited and translated by David McI. Gracie. Cambridge, Mass.: Cowley Publications, 1986.

The *Dietrich Bonhoeffer Werke* (volumes 1-17) is now complete and is being translated into English by the International Bonhoeffer Society–English Language Section through Fortress Press (Minneapolis) as the *Dietrich Bonhoeffer Works*. This critical English edition is projected to be completed by the year 2008.

For an ongoing and updated record of what is known to be published in the English language relating to the legacy of Dietrich Bonhoeffer, consult the annual *Bibliographical Update* that is printed in the *Newsletter* of the International Bonhoeffer Society–English Language Section; this update is a supplement to the *Bonhoeffer Bibliography: Primary Sources and Secondary Literature in English* (published through the American Theological Library Association) by Wayne Whitson Floyd and Clifford J. Green in 1992).

Secondary Resources for Further Study

Depending on the depth of one's interest in further study of Bonhoeffer's legacy, the following English-language resources are suggested:

Dietrich Bonhoeffer: A Spoke in the Wheel, by Renate Wind (Grand Rapids: Eerdmans, 1991), is an excellent book that familiarizes the reader with Bonhoeffer's life, writings, and the persons closest to him in family and faith. (182 pages)

Dietrich Bonhoeffer — A Biography, by Eberhard Bethge (revised edition by Victoria Barnett published by Fortress Press in 2000), remains the definitive biography (1,048 pages) written by Bonhoeffer's close friend who later married Bonhoeffer's niece, Renate Schleicher. Bethge was entrusted with the literary and theological legacy, first editing *Die Mündige Welt* (Munich: Christian Kaiser Verlag, beginning in 1956), then the six-volume *Gesammelte Schriften* (Munich: Christian Kaiser Verlag, 1965-74), and recently completing the editorial oversight for the seventeen-volume *Dietrich Bonhoeffer Werke* (Munich: Christian Kaiser Verlag).

The Cup of Wrath, by Mary Glazener (Gracewing of England and Smyth & Helwys of Georgia, 1992 and 1996), is a historical novel of high quality telling in narrative fashion the story of Bonhoeffer's life. (447 pages)

A Testament to Freedom: The Essential Writings of Dietrich Bonhoeffer, edited by Geffrey B. Kelly and F. Burton Nelson (San Francisco: HarperSanFrancisco, 1990), offers readers a representative sample of primary Bonhoeffer texts, with introductions and interpretive paragraphs for grasping the context of each selection. For those desiring a complete picture of Bonhoeffer's thought, this volume is the single most important resource. (579 pages)

The Wisdom and Witness of Dietrich Bonhoeffer, by Wayne W. Floyd (Minneapolis: Fortress Press, 2000), is a small collection of meditations based on Bonhoeffer texts. While brief and very selective, this book offers an inspirational and educational glimpse at significant topics of importance to Bonhoeffer and relevant for us today. (128 pages)

Reflections on Bonhoeffer: Essays in Honor of F. Burton Nelson, edited by Geffrey B. Kelly and C. John Weborg (Chicago: Covenant Publications, 1999), is a collection of writings by friends of Burton Nelson who are scholars of the Bonhoeffer legacy. In this volume the reader gains an understanding not only of aspects of Bonhoeffer's thought, but also of how those thoughts are being employed today in the church. (357 pages)

The Cambridge Companion to Dietrich Bonhoeffer, edited by John W. de Gruchy (Cambridge: Cambridge University Press, 1999), is a collection of articles by a variety of respected scholars who discuss Bonhoeffer's life and legacy, as well as major themes in his theology. (281 pages)

The Cost of Moral Leadership: The Spirituality of Dietrich Bonhoeffer, by

Geffrey B. Kelly and F. Burton Nelson (Grand Rapids: Eerdmans, 2003), is a series of chapters that integrate and amplify
Bonhoeffer's understanding of moral leadership and Christian spirituality. Discussion questions for each chapter conclude the book. (300 pages)

Three classic books on Bonhoeffer's theology that deserve a place in any list of resources are Heinrich Ott's *Reality
and Faith: The Theological Legacy of Dietrich Bonhoeffer* (Philadelphia: Fortress Press, 1972); Andre Dumas's *Dietrich Bonhoeffer:
Theologian of Reality* (New York: Macmillan, 1971); and Ernst
Feil's *The Theology of Dietrich Bonhoeffer* (Philadelphia: Fortress
Press, 1985).

Resources relating to Bonhoeffer's influence on contemporary situations and issues would include: *No Difference in
the Fare: Dietrich Bonhoeffer and the Problem of Racism,* by
Josiah U. Young III (Grand Rapids: Eerdmans, 1998); *Bonhoeffer and South Africa: Theology in Dialogue,* by John W. de
Gruchy (Grand Rapids: Eerdmans, 1984); and *Dietrich
Bonhoeffer: His Significance for North Americans,* by Larry Rasmussen (Minneapolis: Fortress Press, 1990).

Other recent books translated into English from a new
generation of Bonhoeffer scholars in Europe include: *Waiting
for the Word,* by the Dutch theologian Frits de Lange (Grand
Rapids: Eerdmans, 2000); *Karl Barth in the Theology of Dietrich
Bonhoeffer,* by Andreas Pangritz of Aachen, Germany (Grand
Rapids: Eerdmans, 2000); *A Theology of Life: Dietrich Bonhoeffer's Religionless Christianity,* by Ralf K. Wüstenberg of Hei-
delberg, Germany (Grand Rapids: Eerdmans, 1998).

Should one choose to pursue in greater detail topics regarding Christian ethics in Bonhoeffer's works, one would be directed to such books as: *Shaping the Future: The Ethics of Dietrich Bonhoeffer* (Philadelphia: Fortress Press, 1985) and *Consequences* (Minneapolis: Fortress Press, 1999), both by James H. Burtness; *Ethical Responsibility: Bonhoeffer's Legacy to the Churches,* edited by John D. Godsey and Geffrey B. Kelly (Lewiston, N.Y.: Edwin Mellen Press, 1981); *Theology and the Practice of Responsibility: Essays on Dietrich Bonhoeffer,* edited by Wayne W. Floyd, Jr., and Charles Marsh (Valley Forge, Pa.: Trinity Press International, 1994); *Christian Faith and Public Choices: The Social Ethics of Barth, Brunner and Bonhoeffer,* by Robin W. Lovin (Philadelphia: Fortress Press, 1984); *Bonhoeffer's Ethics: Old Europe and New Frontiers,* edited by Guy Carter, René van Eyden, Hans-Dirk Van Hoogstraten, and Jürgen Wiersma (Kampen, the Netherlands: Kok Pharos, 1991).

A very valuable resource written by Sabine Leibholz-Bonhoeffer (Dietrich's twin sister) is *The Bonhoeffers: Portrait of a Family* (Chicago: Covenant Publications, 1994). After very interesting descriptions of the eight Bonhoeffer children, Frau Leibholz tells the story of her family's life before, during, and after their forced emigration to England in 1938 because of her husband Gerhardt's Jewish genealogy.